Better Homes and Gardens®

Fences
& Gates

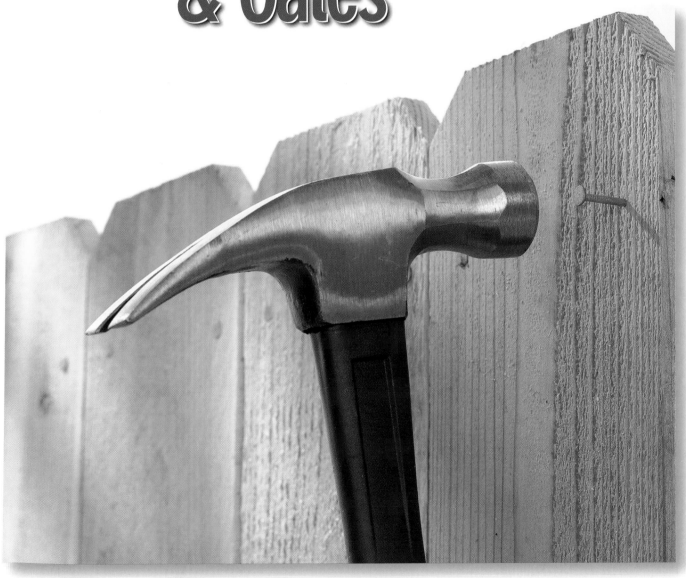

Meredith® Books
Des Moines, Iowa

Table of Contents

PLANNING AND DESIGNING A FENCE

Defining spaces 6
Creating security 8
Increasing privacy 10
Tempering the environment................... 12
Designing gates 14

MATERIALS AND TOOLS

Essential tools 18
Landscaping tools 22
Choosing lumber 24
Synthetic, vinyl, and metal fencing............. 27
Hardware and latches 28
Fasteners and hardware 30

BASIC BUILDING TECHNIQUES

Measuring and marking 32
Using a circular saw.......................... 34
Fastening.................................... 36
Cutting notches, mortises, and tenons........ 40
Laying out a fence and setting posts.......... 42
Laying out a curved fence line 47
Laying out sloped fences 48
Building an edge-rail fence frame.............. 50
Building a flat-rail frame 52
Installing surface-mounted infill............... 54
Installing inset infill.......................... 56
Infill installation tips 58
Building curved fence sections 59
Dealing with obstacles........................ 60

BUILDING FENCES

Vertical board fence 62
Horizontal rail fence 66
Basket-weave fence 70
Louvered fence 72
Mortised post-and-rail fence.................. 74
Picket fence.................................. 76
Lattice fence 79
Siding fence 82
Prefabricated panel fence..................... 86
Ornamental metal fence...................... 88
Vinyl and synthetic fence 92
Chain-link fence 96
Virginia zigzag fence......................... 100
Kentucky rail fence 102
Bamboo fence 104
Variations on fence style..................... 106

Building Gates

Building a braced-frame gate 110

Building a Z-frame gate 112

Building a diagonal solid-core gate 114

Building a paneled gate 116

Hanging a gate 118

Repairing and Maintaining Fences and Gates

Repairing rails 122

Adding posts 124

Replacing posts 126

Shoring up a damaged post 128

Straightening a leaning fence 130

Fixing sagging gateposts 132

Repairing gates 134

Choosing finishes for outdoor projects 137

Glossary 139

Index 141

Better Homes and Gardens® Fences and Gates
Editor: Larry Johnston
Copy Chief: Terri Fredrickson
Copy Editor: Kevin Cox
Publishing Operations Manager: Karen Schirm
Senior Editor, Asset and Information Management: Phillip Morgan
Edit and Design Production Coordinator: Mary Lee Gavin
Art and Editorial Sourcing Coordinator: Jackie Swartz
Editorial Assistant: Kaye Chabot
Book Production Managers: Pam Kvitne, Marjorie J. Schenkelberg,
　Mark Weaver
Imaging Center Operator: Chris Sprague
Contributing Copy Editor: Andrea Kline
Contributing Proofreaders: David Craft, Heidi Johnson, Nancy Ruhling
Contributing Technical Proofreader: Barbara L. Klein
Contributing Indexer: Don Glassman
Other Contributors: Janet Anderson

Additional Editorial Contributions from
**　Abramowitz Creative Studios**
Publishing Director/Designer: Tim Abramowitz
Designer: Kelly Bailey
Designer: Joel Wires
Photography: Image Studios
　Account Executive: Lisa Egan
　Photographer: Bill Rein
　Assistant: Rick Nadke
Illustrator: Dave Brandon

Meredith® Books
Editor in Chief: Gregory H. Kayko
Executive Director, Design: Matt Strelecki
Managing Editor: Amy Tincher-Durik
Executive Editor/Group Manager: Benjamin W. Allen
Senior Associate Design Director: Tom Wegner
Marketing Product Manager: Brent Wiersma

Executive Director, Marketing and New Business: Kevin Kacere
Director, Marketing and Publicity: Amy Nichols
Executive Director, Sales: Ken Zagor
Director, Operations: George A. Susral
Director, Production: Douglas M. Johnston
Business Director: Jim Leonard

Senior Vice President: Karla Jeffries
Vice President and General Manager: Douglas J. Guendel

Meredith Publishing Group
President: Jack Griffin
Executive Vice President: Doug Olson

Meredith Corporation
Chairman of the Board: William T. Kerr
President and Chief Executive Officer: Stephen M. Lacy

In Memoriam: E.T. Meredith III (1933–2003)

Photography Courtesy of:
Photographers credited may retain copyright © to the
listed photographs:

California Redwood Association
Photo by Andrew McKinney
www.calredwood.org
Page 114 - T

L = Left, R = Right, C = Center, B = Bottom, T = Top

All of us at Meredith® Books are dedicated to providing
you with the information and ideas you need to enhance
your home and garden. We welcome your comments and
suggestions. Write to us at:
Meredith Books
Home Improvement Books Department
1716 Locust St.
Des Moines, IA 50309–3023

Note to the Readers: Due to differing conditions, tools,
and individual skills, Meredith Corporation assumes
no responsibility for any damages, injuries suffered, or
losses incurred as a result of following the information
published in this book. Before beginning any project,
review the instructions carefully, and if any doubts or
questions remain, consult local experts or authorities.
Because codes and regulations vary greatly, you always
should check with authorities to ensure that your project
complies with all applicable local codes and regulations.
Always read and observe all of the safety precautions
provided by manufacturers of any tools, equipment,
or supplies, and follow all accepted safety procedures.

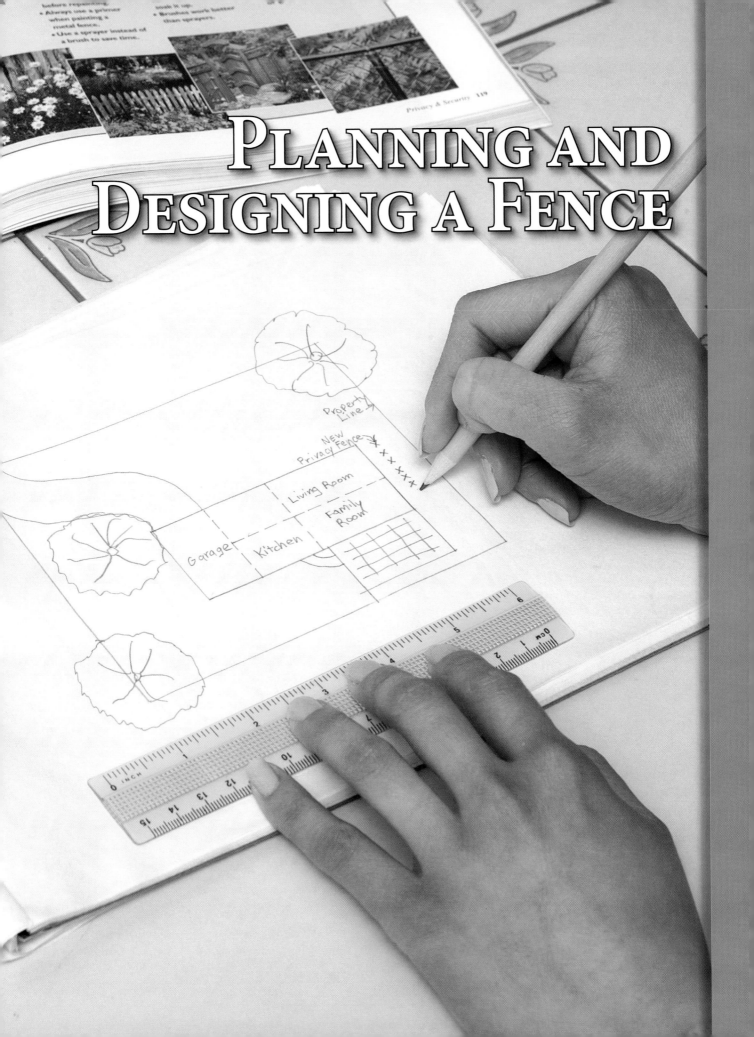

PLANNING AND DESIGNING A FENCE

Defining spaces

Defining property boundaries is the original role of fencing. If that is your first priority, the style you decide to build will depend on whether you are planning a front yard fence or a backyard fence.

Front yard fences

Front yard fences traditionally define the extent of the property and provide some (but not complete) security. Front yard fences usually aren't required to provide much privacy; if anything their role is to be inviting. The best fences emphasize particular features of the house or landscape to enhance the home and its neighborhood.

Front yard fences usually are shorter than those around backyards—3 to 4 feet is typical—but you often can produce a striking effect by building a taller or lower one. Or a fence can carry the color of the house or a design feature into the yard.

Defining a space may require only erecting a low or open fence. Where security, privacy, or containment is not a priority, rail fences are good for the front edge of the yard. Rail fences—even those that look hand-hewn and rustic—go well with most houses. To accent the yard boundary or call attention to a corner planting bed, build a simple corner rail.

Setting bounds
A gracefully curved fence separates the patio from the yard but doesn't isolate either thanks to the open infill design. A low fence is an effective way to define any area but leave it accessible.

Picket, chain-link, and ornamental metal fences are common lot line fences for homeowners who want more containment and security. They can help prevent children and animals from running into or out of the yard and lend some additional security. Solid board fences provide the most security, but a tall board fence around the front yard can be severe; keep the height low. You can use any fencing suitable for installations 3 to 4 feet high.

Backyard fences

In backyards, boundary marking takes on a different look because a fence needs to function as a lot line marker and provide security and privacy as well. In many neighborhoods you won't need to be as concerned with neighborhood styles in back as in your front yard.

A board fence, in any of its numerous styles and variations, is the right choice for many backyards.

PINPOINT THE PROPERTY LINE

Before you build a fence along your lot line, make sure you know exactly where the line is—along its entire length and on all sides of your property. Locating the lot line markers may take a little detective work.

Start by looking for metal spikes or stakes. They may be buried—if they ever have been put in. If they're not visible rent a metal detector to try to find them.

When you locate them replace each one with a 2-foot length of 1-inch galvanized pipe driven to within 1 inch of grade. This way you can see them later and the mower blade won't hit them. Locate all the stakes; don't assume your lot lines are laid out in straight lines or right angles. A misplaced fence section invites trouble with neighbors and could lead to legal action.

If you can't find the lot line markers, hire a surveyor. It will cost a few hundred dollars, but you'll avoid conflict with your neighbors and save the additional money you might have to spend to relocate the fence.

Privacy without confinement
This tall fence provides privacy for a patio. Open latticework in the top and randomly spaced fence boards relieve the fortress effect.

Board fences, along with paling, stake, and siding fences, work well to combine lot line definition with security and privacy. Combine any of these materials with lattice or louver panels—either as infill, as a top panel, or both—to keep the fence from being too confining.

Separating areas

Lot lines aren't the only boundaries that need definition. Areas inside your yard often need to be separated. Fences can keep work areas from visually spilling into recreation areas; they can separate storage space from relaxation retreats, entertainment areas from garden plots.

Small versions of the rail fence, for example, will separate your garden from other areas of your yard. If you build a low fence with benches, you'll make your gardening more convenient and comfortable. Low fences should be between 12 and 24 inches high.

Tall screens built from stakes, lattice, and other materials with open patterns are effective at hiding unattractive items—garbage cans or an unsightly metal storage shed. Or you can conceal them behind a vine-covered trellis— a fencelike structure.

Out of sight
This lattice fence screens air-conditioning equipment from view. A gate provides easy access for maintenance. The screen also protects the equipment from damage.

Lath or lattice panels 3 to 4 feet tall can screen the garden in the winter and provide a year-round accent. Wire-bound slat fencing doesn't have to be permanent. Roll it and wire it to metal posts so it's out of the way during the planting and growing seasons. Unroll it in the winter.

FIND OUT WHAT'S BELOW

Do you know what's under the ground you want to dig into or run a fence across? Perhaps it's your water line or telephone connection. If you're not sure of the location of all your utility lines—sewer, water, electrical, telephone, gas, and TV cable— call each utility company. Most utility firms will flag the location of their lines at no cost. Leave the flags in until your planning is done and be sure to mark the line locations on your property plat map. Be specific—include depths and exact distances from structures and other reference points.

Feature fence
This fence is practical and enhances the landscape. It hides a utility area and offers seating plus a cozy nook with a table for two.

CODES AND COVENANTS

Before you start your fence planning—or at least early in the process—visit your local building department to find out about local regulations that govern fences. You're likely to run into one or more of the following:

- Building Codes: Almost all communities establish local codes that govern how residential structures should be built. These codes set standards for safety regarding materials and construction methods. Some building codes specify the materials that you can use to build residential fences.
- Zoning Ordinances: Zoning ordinances govern the use of property and establish maximum heights for structures (including fences) as well as how far they can be located from other properties (a distance called the setback). In many communities zoning laws may prohibit certain materials and fence heights at the setback line but allow the same materials farther in from the property line.
- Covenants and Deed Restrictions: Communities and neighborhoods may set restrictions in property deeds to maintain neighborhood property values or to preserve specific architectural and historical styles. Such covenants may limit fence materials and locations.

Most municipalities have appeal procedures for codes, ordinances, and covenants. These procedures won't guarantee you'll be granted an exception (a variance), but they ensure that your request will be heard.

After you've researched the restrictions that will affect your fence, incorporate them into your planning.

Creating security

A security fence is most often thought of as a structure intended to keep people or things out. But it also can be built to keep people or things in—or both. Depending on the purpose of a security fence, construction and materials can vary widely.

Keeping things in

If your primary goal is containing toddlers in a play area, chain-link or wire-mesh fence with a 2-inch opening is excellent material. Each offers sufficient height (at least 4 feet) and continuous visibility, allowing parents to keep an eye on their children's play.

A toddlerproof fence will not necessarily keep older children from straying however. Chain link especially will give children toeholds for climbing as they grow taller and more adventuresome.

Chain link and wire mesh are also effective for containing smaller pets (see "Keep the Dogs In," below right). And metal is a better material than wood because dogs can't gnaw or scratch through it.

Containing larger animals—such as horses—in rural areas requires wire, panel, or rail fencing that is not covered in this book. Consult a local agricultural extension agent for information about these fences.

Keeping things out

Fencing designed to keep children or pets in will usually also keep children or pets out. If keeping intruders out is your

Solid but with a soft side

A traditional tall board fence offers security with privacy, but a long expanse of solid fencing can overwhelm adjacent spaces. Plants espaliered on the fence break up the expanse and soften the look.

SPECIFICATIONS FOR SECURITY

Don't let your security fence create insecurity. Many urban residents find that the fence they built to keep out burglars offers intruders cover from watchful neighbors or passersby once the fence is scaled or breached.

A good security fence permits adequate visibility from the outside (wrought iron, tubular steel, and chain link are good choices). It should also be high enough to discourage prowlers (5 feet is a minimum; 6 feet or more is better if the style of the fence will not be compromised), tough enough to resist break-ins (wood is adequate; metal is better), and difficult to climb (no surfaces for handholds or footholds).

Designed for dogs

Iron fence sections, heavy posts, and a digproof zone of stones and concrete rubble along the bottom keep these dogs contained.

KEEP THE DOGS IN

Before you install a dog fence, answer these questions:
- How high can your dog jump?
- How deep can your dog dig?

If your dog is a puppy, answer the questions based on its mature size.

The fence should be at least a couple of inches higher than the pet can jump—as a general rule, 6 feet high for larger dogs and 4 feet high for smaller dogs—and buried 6 inches to discourage tunneling.

You can avoid the need to build a dogproof fence by using electronic fencing. Sold as invisible dog fencing, these systems rely on a buried wire and a collar worn by the dog. When the dog strays beyond the border of the wire, the collar senses it and gives the dog a mild shock. If your dog is particularly nervous or aggressive, however, the shock may not deter it and you will have to rely on building a barrier.

Drowning is the second leading cause of accidental death of children under 3 years.

If you have a swimming pool, make sure that its fence won't let unattended children in. Build it so children can't climb over or under it or slip through its infill.

The fence should allow clear visibility from the outside into the pool area—chain link, pickets, and clear acrylic are good choices. Tall, closely spaced ornamental metal fencing offers a stylish alternative that is difficult to climb.

Gates should be self-closing and self-latching, and their construction should match the safety requirements of the fencing.

Check with your local building department for code requirements that are likely to contain measures at least as strict as those established for swimming pools by the American Fence Association and the U.S. Consumer Products Safety Commission. Don't overlook your spa or garden pond—many communities define these as installations that require a fenced enclosure.

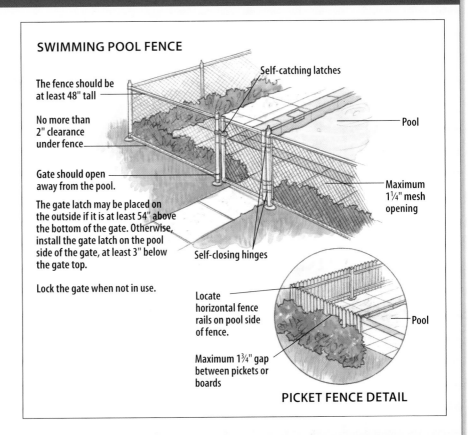

SWIMMING POOL FENCE

The fence should be at least 48" tall

No more than 2" clearance under fence

Gate should open away from the pool.

The gate latch may be placed on the outside if it is at least 54" above the bottom of the gate. Otherwise, install the gate latch on the pool side of the gate, at least 3" below the gate top.

Lock the gate when not in use.

Self-catching latches

Pool

Maximum 1¼" mesh opening

Self-closing hinges

Locate horizontal fence rails on pool side of fence.

Maximum 1¾" gap between pickets or boards

Pool

PICKET FENCE DETAIL

priority, both the strength of your fence and its dimensions will change.

A security fence to keep out intruders should be tall, sturdy, and hard to climb. Although chain link often is used for security fencing, the solid board or siding fence styles shown on pages 62–65 and 82–85 provide an additional psychological deterrent—they may prove more effective simply because intruders can't see what's on the other side.

Solid fences built primarily for security also provide complete privacy. But a secure enclosure comes with a price—it can feel confining.

To open the confinement build see-through panels (small lattice windows, for example) in board or siding fencing. Use the panel framing shown on page 81 or modify some of the sections so they contain infill that isn't solid. Your design will be stylish and you'll avoid feeling like a prisoner of your own security project.

Before you finalize your security fence design, research lighting and alarm systems. With motion-sensing lights and an alarm system that fits your lifestyle and budget, you can keep your property secure without having your fence as your only security feature.

Deer are lovely, graceful—and voracious. They often have the same taste in flowers and landscape plantings that you do.

If your garden is small, a short fence may do the trick—deer, like people, don't like confined spaces. They don't like noise, either, so some gardeners have eliminated deer feeding by tying plastic grocery bags to rope or wire strung between posts. No matter what you do, clear tall brush and weeds away from the perimeter of your garden fence.

The most effective way to keep deer out is to build something they're not hungry enough to jump over. A 5-foot fence will hold back deer looking for a snack, but if deer food in the wild is in short supply, nothing less than 8 feet will do. If stylishness isn't necessary but economy is, string 4-inch woven wire or poultry wire between metal T-posts.

The smaller wire mesh will also keep out burrowing pests. Space the posts (use 4×4s at the corners) 10 feet apart, wire the fencing to the posts, and stake or bury the bottom.

Increasing privacy

Of all the reasons for building a fence, establishing privacy is most often ranked highest by landscape architects. That's because most people use their yard more often and enjoy it more if they don't feel they're on display.

If you find yourself waving at your neighbors every time you're out in your own backyard, it's a sure sign that one or both of you should start planning for privacy.

Solid fences, total privacy

Blocking a view creates privacy. For privacy that's immediate and total, erect a tall wooden fence. Such fences are typically about 6 feet high (many communities prohibit fences that are higher). Consider board fences, siding fences, paling fences, and slats. A basket-weave fence functions well as a privacy screen and offers some protection from the wind.

Solid fencing that provides total privacy has some drawbacks. If the fence stretches for a long distance, it tends to be imposing and confining—especially in a narrow city yard. Also, if it's tall enough to provide the privacy you want, it may also cast total shade where you need dappled shade or no shade at all.

Screen play
A tall lattice fence veils the view into and out of this yard, making it feel more private without seeming solitary.

A tall, solid fence will also create strong downdrafts on the sheltered side instead of blocking the wind (see pages 12–13). And although the fence provides privacy, it also obstructs any desirable views you might have from inside the yard.

To solve these problems you might be able to build solid fencing along only part of the lot line. At the point from which you could be observed, study the patio or other area in which you need privacy. One bay of solid fencing that blocks the neighbors' angle of view

CONTROL NOISE WITH FENCES

Noise is as much of an intrusion on your privacy as are peering eyes. When it comes to noise control, the general rule is that the thicker and more dense the material, the more effective it is in muffling sound.

Solid masonry walls are perhaps the best structures to install if noise control is your greatest landscaping need. A wall is expensive, however, and may not be in keeping with your overall landscape design or your budget.

Don't expect solid board or board-on-board fences to do the job; their flat, hard surfaces don't absorb much sound. You can improve their effectiveness, however, by planting shrubs, vines, or other vegetation.

Board-and-batten and featherboard fences are more effective. Their surfaces have irregular planes that break up the sound waves and scatter them.

Plywood and tongue-and-groove fences are slightly better, but high shingle and clapboard fences will do the best job. These fences are built over an enclosure that acts as an air chamber that absorbs some of the sound, while the shingle or clapboard surface deflects it.

Simple shield
This striking fence of horizontal boards shields the garden seating area from wind and neighbors' eyes.

may be all you need. To create privacy in a single section of a fence that runs the length of your lot line, build tall sections where you want total privacy and short sections where you want to preserve the view. Or you can install lattice sections (or clear materials, such as acrylic) in the solid infill to let the views in where privacy is not needed. Such variations allow the fence (and you) to breathe.

Louvers and lattice

Vertical louvers and lattice can be perfect privacy fences because they screen views from the outside without creating a feeling of confinement.

These fences break up the lines of sight, calling attention to themselves without completely blocking the views beyond. You get privacy without complete obstruction and without feeling you're hemmed in by a stockade.

Visibility through vertical louvers or lattice is usually not good enough to see what's going on behind the fence because the eye usually focuses on the solid surfaces. (The privacy afforded by vertical louvers breaks down near streets—people in cars that pass by at just the right speed can see through the fence.) Horizontal louvers block views entirely.

Cut it out

Boards of alternating height stop short of the cap railing to give this tall fence an airy look. Cutouts in the boards form a window and random viewpoints (inset) while maintaining privacy.

Privacy by degree

Although it's usual to think of privacy in terms limited to completely blocking views, don't stop there. Just as rooms in the interior of your home have different privacy levels, so can different areas of your landscape.

You may need a tall fence to make a courtyard or patio private, but 4-foot bamboo or open-face grape-stake sections will more subtly seclude

a backyard retreat. A 6-foot stockade may be fine for the perimeter of your yard, but low lattice panels with meandering morning glories will screen a utility area.

Lattice also works nicely overhead. Supported by posts and laced with vines, it will block views from above—perfect for tight-fitting urban yards with neighboring apartments or multistory structures.

All shelter, no privacy

Privacy is less of a concern than preserving the view from this patio, so the windscreen is plastic glazing material. Plate glass would be hazardous.

FENCING SLOPES AND OBSTACLES

Don't let slopes and obstacles (trees, rocks, gullies, and banks) get in the way of your fencing plans. Make them part of your design.

You can remove trees, of course, but removal is costly and disruptive. Besides, it's not your only option. Build a curved fence portion around the tree (see pages 47 and 59) or stop the fence on one side of the tree and start it on the other (see page 60).

The same is true for large rocks; they are often part of Mother Nature's original landscape design and can become an important accent with construction techniques that highlight them. If your fence runs along the back edge of one of these accents of nature, change the infill material (or its pattern) behind the rock to show it off.

You can fill a recess in grade by extending the infill down to just above grade level, but building fences next to banks, steep slopes, and cliffs is more complicated. Consult a landscape architect to see whether you'll need to build a retaining wall—not the kind of incorporation into the landscape you want—to keep your fence from eventually washing away.

Tempering the environment

Fences make a landscape much more comfortable and enjoyable. They provide shade, help light up dark areas, and reduce strong winds to gentle breezes.

As you conduct your inventory of fencing needs, take into account sun and wind patterns in your yard and identify areas that could use protection. Note those places on your sketches.

Study first, build later

Your yard is full of microclimates—small areas where temperature, sun patterns, and wind velocities differ from general conditions.

If you want fencing to increase shade, plot the course of the sun across your yard. Stake out shade patterns at different times of the day. Remember that the angle of the sun changes with the seasons. The winter sun is low in the southern horizon, so it casts shadows during much of the day. In the summer, shade can all but disappear from 10 a.m. to 3 p.m.

Include prevailing winds as well as seasonal breezes in your wind study. Prevailing winds blow from the same general direction over your region. Seasonal breezes are more localized and occur only at specific times of the day, intermittently during a season.

WINDSCREEN/FENCE HEIGHTS

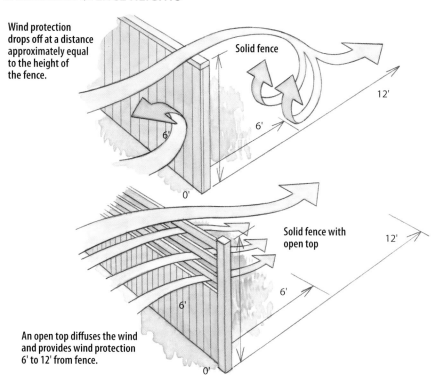

Wind protection drops off at a distance approximately equal to the height of the fence.

Solid fence

An open top diffuses the wind and provides wind protection 6' to 12' from fence.

Solid fence with open top

Streamers tied to stakes will help reveal changing wind currents in your yard.

Fencing with the sun

The amount of shade a fence creates depends on its height, its proximity to the shaded area, and its axis. Tall, solid fencing can shade nearby decks, patios, or garden plots with special plants that require only partial shade. Lattice panels make dappled shade; acrylic panels will let in all the sunlight. If you

THE SUN'S SEASONAL CHANGES

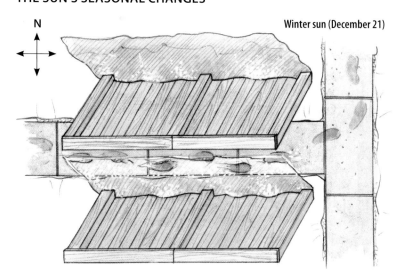

N

Winter sun (December 21)

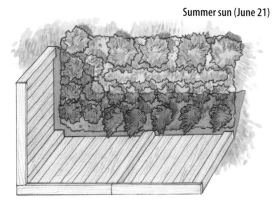

Summer sun (June 21)

A fence south of a sidewalk (left) blocks low winter sun and could lead to ice hazards; moving it to the north side, if possible, is better. Fencing the south and west sides of a garden (above) makes partial shade for plants.

Teamwork
This fence clearly defines a border and prevents casual entry yet it doesn't block sun and air from the plants on the other side. The plants in turn contribute to its effectiveness as a windbreak and enhance privacy in the yard.

need constant shade throughout the year on the north side, build the fence on an east-west axis.

Fences will reflect light too. If you paint the sunlit side of your fence with a light color, sunlight (and heat) will bounce into a nearby planting bed—a useful tool for gardeners whose spring plantings might be ruined by a late frost. A fence built to improve privacy will send warm light into a nearby south-facing room if you paint it a light color.

Controlling the wind

Wind—like water—takes the path of least resistance. It spills over objects and creates microconditions in your landscape. Fences can adjust these conditions to your benefit.

For example, wind that blows across a patio surface and into the corner of the house creates eddies that swirl and dump debris before they move on. You can control the prevailing wind to minimize the effect of those eddies, but don't expect a solid fence to help much. Wind-control research shows that wind swirls over the top of solid objects and drops back down at a distance roughly equal to the height of the fence. (See the illustration on page 12.) Solid fences create low-pressure pockets that pull the wind down into the area you want protected.

Fences that divert or break up the wind provide better wind control. A louvered fence changes the direction of the wind and mitigates the debris-filled eddies noted above.

Fences with gaps or openings in the surface, such as board on board, grape stakes, spaced slats, basket weave, or lattice, filter the wind and slow it so it passes through in a pleasant breeze. A solid surface that blocks the wind would cause it to vault over the fence and blow down the other side with turbulence.

Breezy boards
Spaced boards with decorative cutouts make this fence a wind screen rather than a barrier. The open top helps control the wind too.

SNOW FENCES

Snow fence design—the object of substantial research over the last 30 years—has become a science in itself. Here are the three types:

- **Plastic snow fence:** Introduced in the 1960s, plastic snow fence is effective at containing snow. It has a serviceable life span of five years (longer if taken down between seasons) but requires considerable maintenance.
- **Lath fence:** Also called Canadian or "cribbed" fence, it's made of 1½-inch lath wired in 25- or 50-foot rolls. It's longer-lived but not as effective as plastic or Wyoming snow fence.
- **Wyoming snow fence:** Made of 1×6s spaced 6 inches apart, starting 10 inches above the ground, Wyoming snow fence will last 25 years or more, is as effective as plastic, and requires minimum maintenance.

Snow fence should run in a straight line, parallel to and centered on the area that you want to protect. It's best to orient it perpendicular to the prevailing winds and at a distance from the protected area equal to roughly 30 times its height.

Designing gates

A gate does more than just open or close a gap in a fence. It can also serve as a focal point, punctuate an entry, or highlight a special area.

First impressions

Gates create an image and project an impression about what lies beyond. A tall locked gate does not invite entrance. Low, painted pickets, on the other hand, are more welcoming. Gates can be strictly utilitarian, architectural, or whimsical.

Although a gate may be the last element you build in the fence, think about it early in the planning. You should decide at least three things about the gate or gates before you finalize your fence line: location, size, and direction of swing.

Common sense will help decide the gate's location. It should be convenient to natural traffic paths. Determine the size of the gate by what will pass through it (see "Guidelines for Gate Openings" on the opposite page). Direction of swing depends on where you place the gate.

Then keep your overall fence style—and the following pointers—in mind as you begin to make decisions about the appearance of your gate.

Gates: architectural to whimsical

A pergola over a pair of arch-top gates creates a dignified portal while the rustic gate (inset) makes a far less formal entry. You can design a gate to fit your home, fence, landscape, and personal style.

Function and materials

A main entry gate deserves more prominence than one leading into a service yard. Materials and how you combine them are important factors in achieving the look you want.

A gate that contrasts with the fence in style or material becomes a focal point. To downplay a gate, design it to match the fence. Making the gate less noticeable often enhances the feeling of privacy. Special effects—such as distinguishing trim—invite attention to a gate without detracting from the continuity of the fence line. An arbor or canopy can further set off an entry.

A GATE AS A STRUCTURAL SYSTEM

Gates, like fences, form a structural system. Regardless of style, each gate is basically a frame with infill. Bracing is frequently an essential part of gate design. A diagonal brace can transfer some load from the top of the gate to the frame side and post. The strength of a gate depends on its structural design as well as the quality of its materials and construction.

Gates place a heavy load on their posts. Gateposts are typically larger and are set deeper than other fence posts to support the load.

Join the parts of the system with hardware of the appropriate size that matches the style of the fence. Latches, catches, hinges, and other accessories provide more than their mechanical functions. They are also part of the aesthetics of a gate.

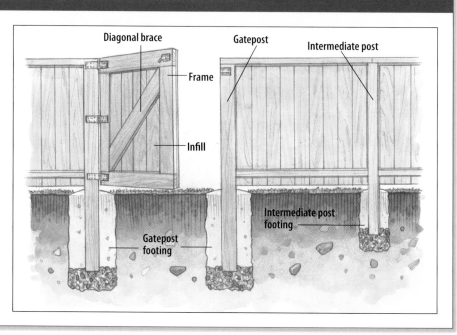

Diagonal brace · Gatepost · Intermediate post · Frame · Infill · Intermediate post footing · Gatepost footing

Designing the gate

A gate must swing open and shut smoothly and look good for many years. For a gate to do its job well, these three elements must work together:

Structure: It takes sound framing and bracing, solid joints, and properly installed infill to make a durable gate. A gate that's too wide will probably sag, and an overly heavy one can put an unnecessary—often damaging—burden on the hardware.

Hardware: Rustproof fasteners— stainless-steel screws are best—plus stout hinges, latches, catches, and locks are essential to ensure a gate's utility, appearance, and durability. Buy hardware, especially hinges, adequate for the size and weight of your gate. Attach hardware securely with screws.

Gateposts: Gateposts must be set sufficiently deep in stable footings to transfer the load of the gate to the ground. Because gateposts must support the weight of the gate and withstand the forces of opening and closing, they are often one size larger than the intermediate fence posts.

As you design your gate, you can leave decisions on style, infill, and other details until last. Plan the structure first, then add the infill later to achieve the right look. Begin with this question: How wide should the gate be?

Opening width

If a gate is too wide, it will soon sag and hang out of square because of its own weight. Tradition says that 4 feet is about the limit for a commonly hinged, one-panel, unsupported gate.

If the fence opening must be wider than 4 feet, you can span the opening with a pair of gates or a single gate with extra support—a wheel at the corner or a diagonal turnbuckle. (See "Guidelines for Gate Openings," below.)

The swing of the gate

To determine which way your gate should swing, look at its surroundings. The illustrations in this section show how the conditions at the location of the gate affect the direction it can swing. Your gate may be able to swing open in both directions. If so, you can purchase special hinges and latches.

Here are some of the more common gate locations and how they affect the swing of the gate:

Boundary line fences: Gates installed along the edge of a property are usually mounted so they swing into the property rather than out across a public sidewalk or into an adjoining property.

In fences that differentiate one part of a property from another, don't rule out hinging a gate to swing both ways, especially if the gate will be in a high-traffic area, such as the walkway leading to a detached garage. A double-swinging gate will save time and trouble when your arms are full of groceries.

Where fences meet: A gate here should be hinged on the side of the section that's nearest the corner of the fence so the swinging gate won't get in the way of views and access through the opening. A two-way gate lends itself well to this kind of opening.

Top or bottom of stairs: If the landing is wider than the arc of the gate's swing, you can safely mount a gate at the top or bottom of a flight of stairs. People need enough space to step back to swing the gate, and the landing forewarns that steps exist beyond. In this situation, the gate can swing in one or both directions.

Along a slope: If you're building a gate on a slope, hinge it on the low side so that as the gate swings open, the bottom will clear the slope. Note that the frame is built square, rather than conforming to the angle of the slope. It breaks the visual line of the fence framework, but the gate gets the structural strength it needs. In this situation the gate can swing in one or both directions.

Across a hillside: Hills, like slopes, require gates to be hung so they will swing out toward the downhill direction; the bottom of the gate will swing free and clear of the slope of the hillside. Gates hung perpendicular to a hill can swing in one direction only.

BOUNDARY LINE FENCES

Designing gates *(continued)*

WHERE FENCES MEET

ALONG A SLOPE

TOP OR BOTTOM OF STAIRS

ACROSS A HILLSIDE

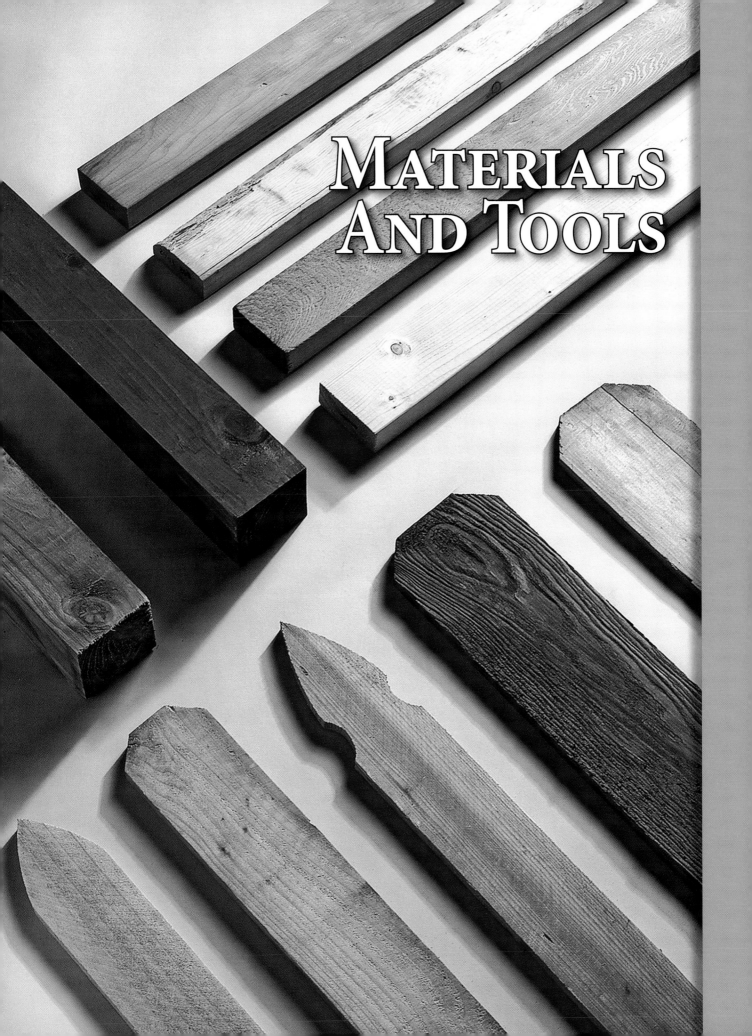

MATERIALS AND TOOLS

Essential tools

Yo may already have all of the tools you'll need to build your fence. If you don't have some of these tools, add them to your tool kit. Most will be handy to have for other projects after the fence is finished so buy high-quality tools. Avoid bargain-price tools, which often break, wear out quickly, don't stay sharp, and may be less comfortable to use.

Layout tools
Layout can be the most exacting aspect of fence building, but layout tools aren't expensive. Here's what you'll need.

Chalkline and chalk
You'll need these to snap straight lines for cuts.

Laser level
A laser level projects plumb and level reference lines onto surfaces.

Line level
This small level hooks to mason's line that can be stretched over distances too long to span with a carpenter's level.

Mason's line
The mainstay of layout work. Use nylon; it doesn't stretch.

Plumb bob
This indicates vertical and helps mark posthole locations.

Steel tape
This is a do-it-yourselfer's constant companion. A 1-inch blade will extend farther without sagging. You'll need at least a 16-footer—a 25-footer will save you time.

Construction tools
The tools in this collection will help you construct a fence from lumber or assemble prefabricated fences.

Adjustable clamp
Handy for holding thick pieces of lumber. Buy several.

Adjustable wrench
Use this to fasten nuts, bolts, and lag screws or to hold a machine-bolt head while you tighten the nut with a socket wrench.

C-clamp
These come in a variety of sizes and handle many jobs. Buy several sizes.

Carpenter's level
Get a 48-inch model for plumbing and leveling. Shorter versions may give false readings over long spans. Buy one with a rigid steel or aluminum frame.

Carpenter's pencil
To avoid endless sharpening and to make visible lines, use a chisel-pointed carpenter's pencil. Buy a sharpener too.

Cat's paw
Makes pulling nails easier.

Caulking gun
Dispenses caulk or adhesive from tubes. Get one with a quick pressure release to save material and reduce the mess.

Combination square
This is an indispensable tool. It helps you check 90- and 45-degree angles quickly, measure depth from surfaces, and lay out cutting lines.

Chisel
Essential for cleaning out notches. Buy high-quality chisels and take good care of them. Drive wood-handle chisels with a mallet, not with a metal hammer. Sharp chisels make clean, accurate cuts. Poorly fitting notches make weak joints.

Circular saw
These come in different sizes. Get a heavy-duty saw with a 7¼-inch carbide-tip combination blade. The extra power will come in handy on this or any other project that requires cutting of framing members.

Cordless drill/driver
This essential tool drills holes and easily drives screws. Buy at least a 14.4-volt model with a spare battery. You'll need spade bits of appropriate sizes for larger holes and to start mortises. Twist drills will drill holes up to ½ inch in diameter for screws and bolts.

Framing hammer
Buy a high-quality, 20-ounce hammer. The extra weight may seem tiring at first, but you'll appreciate it for driving all the nails in a fence.

Framing square
You'll use this large square to square corners and to mark stair stringers.

Groove-joint pliers
Pliers of all types are handy for gripping, holding, and pulling.

Essential tools *(continued)*

Handsaw
You'll need this for quick cuts and to finish some corner cuts where a circular saw won't go.

Jigsaw
If you're cutting patterns on fence boards, you'll need one. Buy a heavy-duty model.

Layout square
This triangular square helps you quickly figure angled cuts or mark cutlines. It's tough and compact and will hold its shape after getting banged around. Some carpenters use this square to guide circular-saw cuts.

Locking pliers
This handy, versatile tool holds, grips, and clamps.

Nail set
Use for setting finishing nails.

Multi-tip screwdriver
Interchangeable tips allow this single screwdriver to drive and remove many kinds of screws.

Plane
Use this tool to shave wood off the edge of a board or to round sharp edges on a post or railing.

Post level
This is a one-purpose tool, but nothing does it better. Strap it to a post to plumb two sides at once.

Power drill
A variable-speed, reversible corded drill is handy for drilling holes in posts.

Pry bar
This is handy when you need to remove nails or force parts into position.

Reciprocating saw
Cuts posts, rustic rails, and other heavy materials. Ideal for cutting set posts to height.

Sawhorses
You'll need at least a pair to support lumber for cutting.

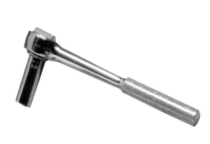

Socket wrench
A ratchet handle and socket is the best tool for tightening nuts and lag screws.

Squeeze clamps
Inexpensive and quick to use, these have plastic pads so they won't dent lumber.

T-bevel
This gauge adjusts to duplicate an angle.

Torpedo level
This short level fits in tighter spaces when a carpenter's level is too long.

Utility knife
Sharpen your pencils and trim some materials with this knife. Buy one with a retractable blade.

Water level
Long-distance leveling is easy and accurate with this tool. Some models attach to the ends of your garden hose.

Landscaping tools

Each of the landscaping tools shown below is indispensable in constructing a fence. Make sure their cutting edges are sharp—tools that cut cleanly through soil and sod will save a great deal of time and effort.

Drain spade: With its narrow, pointed blade, a drain spade is ideal for breaking sod and starting postholes. It also comes in handy for other uses, such as shoveling soil or concrete around posts to set them.

Hand auger: This tool bores holes in the soil with repeated turns of the handle. Set the point in the soil, give it a turn, lift it out of the hole, knock dirt from the blades, and repeat the process until you've reached the depth you want. You can make the job easier by renting a power auger (page 23).

Clamshell posthole digger: A pair of long-handle shovels hinged together offers an efficient way to dig postholes. Open the shovel blades, drive them into the ground, push the handles apart, and lift out a chunk of earth. (You may need to rotate the blades back and forth to cut roots or dislodge small rocks.)

Round-nose shovel: Use this workhorse for all sorts of digging jobs. A long-handle version provides increased leverage. A square-nose spade (not shown) is best for cutting through sod roots if you're removing a large area of turf.

Iron rake: Also known as a bow rake or garden rake, an iron rake breaks up and levels soil.

Tamper: Compact soil around posts and in other spots that require firm, dense earth with a tamper. You can make your own tamper by screwing two 10-inch squares of ¾-inch plywood to one end of a 2×4.

Trowel: Move small amounts of soil in tight spots with this basic gardener's tool. It also comes in handy for cleaning up the sides of postholes and mixing concrete and placing it around posts.

Buying tips

When shopping for tools look them

over critically. Make sure the tool fits you—if a handle is too long or short, try another. Check the quality of the connection between the handle and tool. Look for stout handles or you'll soon end up back at your home center for a more durable model. Handles stamped "hickory" are usually stout.

Most manufacturers offer several lines of tools at various price levels. It's all right to buy an inexpensive version of a tool you'll use rarely, but it's better to spend more on high-quality tools you'll use more frequently.

Caring for landscaping tools
Well-made tools last for years if you don't abuse or neglect them. Here are some maintenance hints:
- Clean tools after each use with a paint stick or steel brush to keep soil from encrusting.
- Wipe wooden handles with linseed oil, then wipe off the excess oil. Paint tools a bright color if you tend to lose them.
- Sharpen tools for efficiency and safety. Usually you can do the job with a metal file.
- Check and tighten all bolts and screws regularly.
- For safety and to maintain cutting edges, hang tools on the wall of your garage or shed. Protect steel blades against rust by applying a light coat of machine oil.

Power posthole diggers

A one-person power auger

You'll need a trailer to haul some models home. Start the engine. Set the bit over the hole and lower it slowly, letting its weight do the work. Raise the bit periodically to clean it. Keep the bit turning when raising it from the hole. Add extensions for deeper holes.

A two-person power auger

Two-person motorized augers are more difficult to operate. Get detailed instructions when renting one. The torque they produce can knock you off balance. Start the engine and plant your (and your helper's) feet firmly before engaging the bit. Be braced for roots and rocks.

A trailer-mounted power auger

This hydraulically powered unit produces maximum boring power with minimum wear and tear on the operator. To ease the auger into the soil, you simply operate a control handle. The hydraulics of the unit do the lifting and lowering.

Choosing lumber

Lumber for a fence must resist rot so use one of these types:

Pressure-treated (PT) lumber, usually pine or fir, is infused with rot-resisting chemicals. It's the least expensive of your choices but pick each board carefully so you get stock that is straight and free of loose knots.

Posts and rails within 6 inches of the soil should be rated for ground contact. Wood that has been kiln-dried after treatment (KDAT) is the highest quality.

Cedar, redwood, and cypress resist rot and insects naturally. But only the heartwood (the centermost core of the tree) is resistant. Seal or stain these woods to keep their natural beauty or let them weather to shades of gray.

A fence that will be painted can be built with pressure-treated wood throughout. If the fence will be stained, you can use pressure-treated lumber for posts and rails and redwood or cedar for the infill to reduce cost.

Lumber is graded for its appearance, strength, and amount of knots. In some species, such as redwood or cedar, some stock is graded for fencing. A lumber grade stamp (page 26) indicates the quality of the stock. If in doubt ask your dealer which lumber is best suited to fencing.

Prebuilt fence panels are available from many lumberyards and home centers. These panels, with rails and infill factory assembled, can save considerable time in fence construction (see pages 86–87). Different styles and wood species usually are available. Inspect panels carefully to ensure that they are soundly built with quality stock.

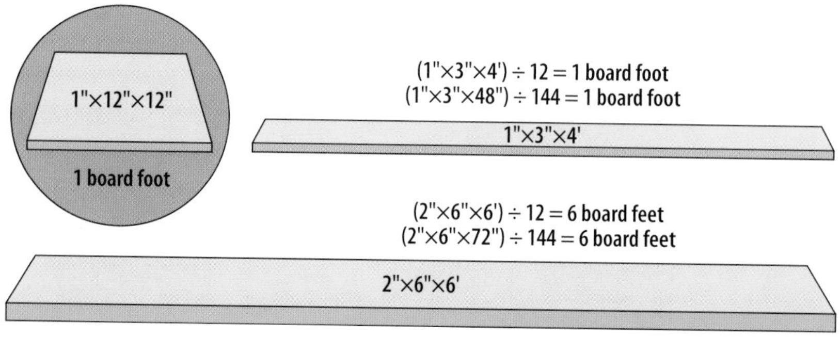

$(1" \times 3" \times 4') \div 12 = 1$ board foot
$(1" \times 3" \times 48") \div 144 = 1$ board foot

1"×12"×12"

1 board foot

1"×3"×4'

$(2" \times 6" \times 6') \div 12 = 6$ board feet
$(2" \times 6" \times 72") \div 144 = 6$ board feet

2"×6"×6'

The board foot

A board foot is a unit of measurement for lumber. To calculate the number of board feet in a board, multiply nominal width by nominal thickness in inches. Then multiply by the actual length in feet and divide by 12 or multiply by the length in inches and divide by 144.

THE REAL SIZE OF LUMBER

Nominal lumber sizes state the dimensions before milling and drying. Actual sizes are smaller. Order lumber by its nominal size. When you measure it you're measuring its actual size.

Nominal	Actual
1×2	¾" × 1½"
1×3	¾" × 2½"
1×4	¾" × 3½"
1×6	¾" × 5½"
1×8	¾" × 7¼"
1×10	¾" × 9¼"
1×12	¾" × 11¼"
2×2	1½" × 1½"
2×4	1½" × 3½"
2×6	1½" × 5½"
2×8	1½" × 7¼"
4×4	3½" × 3½"
6×6	5½" × 5½"

SOME COMMON GRADES OF WOOD

Grade	Characteristics
Clear	Has no knots
Select or select structural	High-quality wood; subdivided into Nos. 1–3 or grades A–D (higher numbers and letters have more knot)
No. 2 common	Has tight knots, no major blemishes; good for shelving
No. 3 common	Some knots may be loose; often blemished or damaged
Construction or standard	Good strength; used for general framing
Utility	Economy grade used for rough framing

MIX AND MATCH

The posts and rails are less visible on some fences, so it really isn't necessary to build the whole fence out of the same kind of wood. The best choice for posts and rails in such a case is usually pressure-treated lumber. You can build the framing with less-expensive treated lumber and spend more on cedar or redwood for infill. If the posts and rails will be visible in your landscape, it may be better to build an unpainted fence entirely with redwood or cedar.

LUMBER SELECTOR

Type		Description	Uses
Pressure-treated lumber		Softwood: tendency to be knotty. Resistant to rot, decay, and insects. Pronounced grain pattern that may raise when wet. Depending on chemical used, freshly treated stock has brown or greenish cast. Can be stained or painted. Weathers to a dull gray.	Posts, rails, painted infill
Cedar		Softwood: can be knotty and tends to split easily. Light pink to brown heartwood is less resistant to rot, decay, and insects than other resistant species but is more durable. Light-color sapwood is not resistant. Rich, light red natural color. Can be stained or painted. Weathers to an attractive gray.	Posts, rails, infill
Redwood		Softwood: Heart redwood is the premium-grade exterior wood: more resistant to rot, decay, and insect damage than cedar but less than cypress. Vertical, even-grain pattern; less susceptible to splitting than cedar. Light cherry red to deep red-brown. Can be stained or painted. Weathers quickly to an attractive gray.	Posts, rails, infill
Cypress		Softwood: native to swampy regions of the southern United States. More rot-, decay-, and insect-resistant than other softwoods. Lightweight, very strong, and durable. Straight-grain pattern. Can be stained or painted. Weathers to a light gray.	Posts, rails, infill

Choosing lumber *(continued)*

How much lumber will you need? The best way to calculate how much you'll need is to draw a dimensioned plan and count the number of posts and rails. Determine the amount of infill material needed for one bay, then multiply by the number of bays. Buy a few more rails and add 10 percent to the infill amount to allow for waste so that you'll get everything you need.

For a solid board fence, you can count framing members and estimate infill by square footage of fence surface.

HANDLING TREATED WOOD

Pressure-treated lumber is saturated with chemical preservatives embedded in the wood's fibers. The industry says that when properly handled, pressure-treated wood is safe and the chemicals will not leach out of the wood. New chemicals are now in use, but existing stock of wood treated with chromated copper arsenate (CCA) still can be sold. When working with pressure-treated lumber, observe the following precautions:

- Wear gloves (except when using power tools).
- Wear a dust mask and goggles when cutting.
- Wash hands before eating, drinking, or smoking.
- Never burn the wood or scraps.
- Dispose of wood scraps with regular trash.
- Don't use the wood indoors.
- Launder work clothes separately from other clothing, especially baby clothing and diapers.

MANAGED FORESTS

Concerned that your lumber may come from irreplaceable forests? Several organizations monitor the forestry industry and promote responsible forest management. For information visit sustainable.org/economy/forestry.html.

HEARTWOOD OR SAPWOOD

Light-color sapwood is less rot-resistant than the darker heartwood. Most boards contain both.

GRADE STAMPS

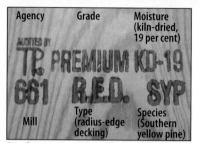

Grade stamps vary. All show wood species, grade, and grading agency. The stamp on pressure-treated lumber shows treatment information as well.

INSPECT BOARDS BEFORE BUYING

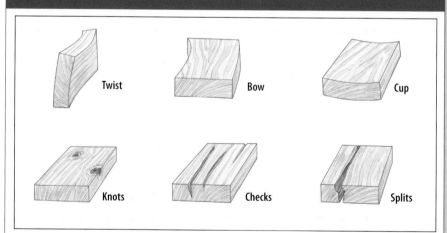

Lumberyards usually have plenty of substandard wood lying around. The best way to be sure you don't get some of it for your fence is to choose the boards yourself. Some lumberyards discourage customers from picking through the stacks because they want to keep wood properly stacked—the only way to keep lumber from warping. But most will let you stand by during selection and reject bad boards. If not, make sure you can return boards that don't meet your standards.

Twisted, bowed, and some cupped boards usually can be brought into line when fastening. Checks are not a structural problem. Checking is often confined to the end of a board so you can cut it off for better appearance. But don't buy split boards. Knots should be tight.

Synthetic, vinyl, and metal fencing

Residential fences are frequently built from wood. But other materials are available and they offer some advantages over wood.

Chain link, for instance, is an inexpensive material for security fencing and vinyl fences require no maintenance over their life. Here are some nonwood materials to consider:

Synthetic

Like decking, synthetic fencing material is made from various recycled products mixed with resins or fiberglass-reinforced resins. These composite materials are usually manufactured in shapes and sizes similar to standard lumber and some have the texture and color of wood. Lattice panels, weaves, and other fencing styles are available. Synthetics come in colors too, so you can build a color fence that will never need painting. Though they don't have the strength of wood or metal, these are durable materials that resist rot.

Because many synthetic materials are like standard lumber in size and shape, you can design and plan a composite fence as easily as a wood one. Composites may be intermixed with standard lumber—composite infill on standard pressure-treated posts and rails for example. Some manufacturers provide prebuilt panels and ready-to-install fence kits too.

Working with synthetics is much like working with wood. You can use standard carpentry tools for cutting and drilling. Screws are used for fastening.

Vinyl

Vinyl and other plastic fencing products are usually sold as complete fence systems or kits. Garden edge fencing is available in snap-together sections or rolls, while taller fences include posts and prefab panels with rails and infill.

Vinyl fences resist rot and moisture damage, but ultraviolet (UV) rays from the sun degrade plastics. Better vinyl fencing has high resistance to UV damage and many products are warranted against it. Some vinyl fences are shiny and white—a good look for a picket fence—and others have wood texture and come in a range of colors.

Vinyl fence assembly details vary among makes and models, but most require setting a starting post and working along the fence line so post spacing will precisely match the panel length (see pages 92–95). A vinyl fence is not as strong as a wood or metal one but is maintenance free.

Parts are precut so there is little cutting to do when assembling a vinyl fence. A handsaw, jigsaw, or circular saw will easily cut the materials when necessary. Some panels can be racked for contour fencing on a slope while others are rigid. Many fences can be installed with no more than a posthole digger, a level, and a cordless drill/driver.

Metal

Metal fencing dates back at least to the industrial age when elegant wrought-iron fences were built around estates, parks, and other proud spaces. Soon black wrought-iron fences were a standard style in cities and towns.

The style is still popular today and is available as preassembled panels that can be installed easily (see pages 88–91). Steel fence panels can be installed with steel posts, between wood posts or masonry pillars, or on top of a low wall. In almost any installation ornamental metal brings elegance and the look of security. It doesn't offer much privacy.

Iron accent
Cast-iron fencing is ideal for garden edging. The finish on this is iron oxide—rust.

Uninterrupted view
Welded-wire field fence provides security along this slope but preserves the view.

Panels are available in several styles from plain square bars to elaborate twisted bars with pike tops. Where prefab panels don't offer the style desired, fabricators can install custom-built ornamental metal fences—but at a price.

Some standard panels can be racked to follow a slope contour. Most metal fences bolt together, and posts must be set one at a time because the panels are a fixed length. Many metal fences are powder-coated to resist rust and require little or no maintenance.

Several styles of bolt-together cast-iron fencing, popular in the Victorian era, are being reproduced today. Original fence sections sometimes turn up in antiques shops and flea markets. Placed most commonly in and around gardens, cast-iron fencing can be painted with bright colors. Left unpainted, iron fencing will rust, which is the look and finish some prefer.

Wire fences are economical and easy to install. Chain link is a popular style for backyards, swimming pools, dog runs, and other installations where security outweighs the need for privacy (see pages 96–99).

Privacy can be enhanced with slats that thread through the fabric, or vines can be trained on the fence for a longer-term solution. Chain link is ideal for some landscape uses because the fence can effectively become invisible against the plants in the background.

Posts, rails, and fence fabric are galvanized to resist rust, and post caps and other hardware are either cast aluminum or galvanized steel. This makes a chain-link fence practically maintenance-free. The fence can be painted with a heavy-nap roller after the galvanizing weathers for a while. Some manufacturers offer vinyl-coated chain-link fencing too.

Hardware and latches

Gate hardware is as much a design element as any other part of the fence or gate structure. Hinges and latches give the gate design a detail or accent that embellishes the appearance of the entire structure. But with gate hardware even the most ornamental parts have a hefty job to do. When you're shopping for hardware, make your choices based on appearance and ruggedness. A durable finish will keep the hardware from rusting quickly.

The many kinds of hinges and latches available almost defy categorization. Many latches are designed for operation from one side only. For example a simple hook-and-eye latch, a slide-action latch, and a striker all operate conveniently from only one side. To open them from the other side of the fence, you have to reach over the top of the gate. A top latch will solve this problem as will a lever-action latch.

Specialty hardware or restoration catalogs are good places to look for attractive or unusual hardware. Ornamental iron shops—or even a brass foundry—will make just about anything you want. You'll pay more, but the cost might be worth it for that one-of-a-kind design. Don't forget antiques shops, salvage yards, and building-material recycling centers.

Latches

Like most aspects of fence planning, it's usually not wise to buy a latch without first considering how easy it is to operate, how securely it closes, and how it fits the style of the gate.

In some cases the gate size will affect your choice of latches. If the gate is tall, for example, and you can't reach over it to get at the latch, you need one that you can operate from both sides.

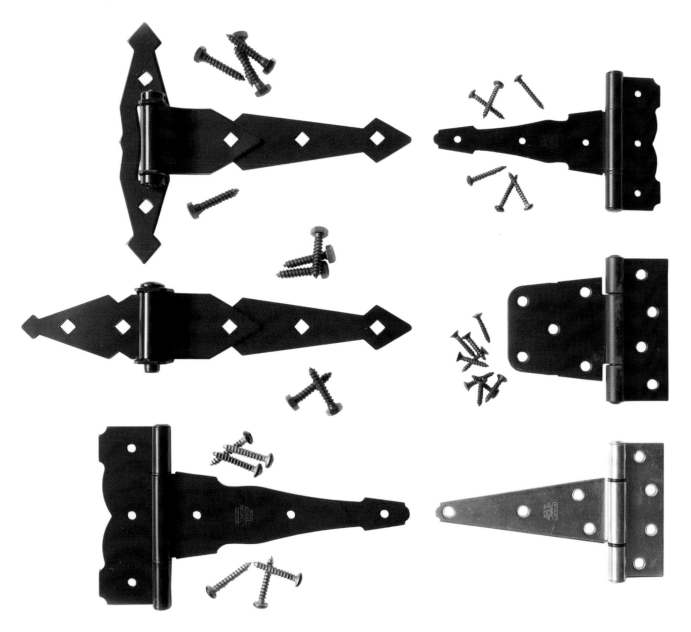

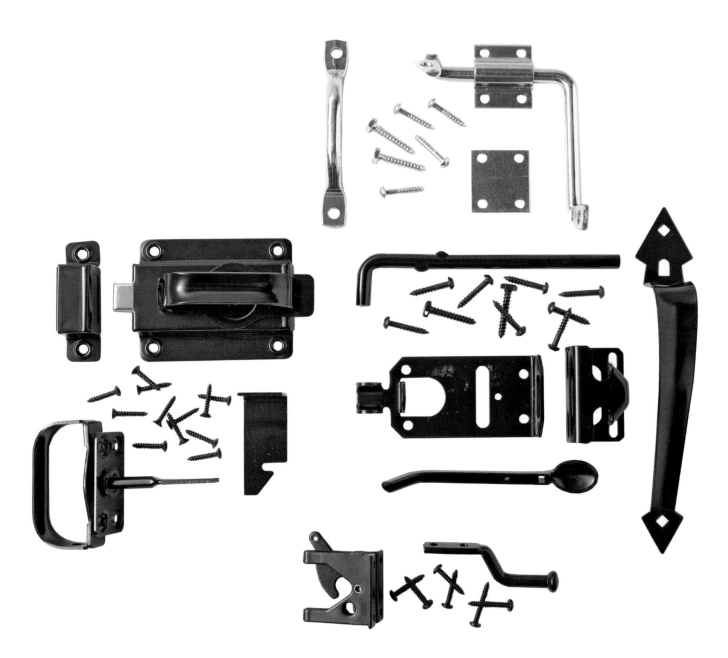

For security some latches include locks or hasps for a padlock. Make sure you can unlock the gate from the inside so getting in or out is easy in an emergency. Check local codes for requirements that apply to gate exit and entry.

Hinges

Even though you can construct a gate from a variety of different materials, there's no such thing as a light gate. By its very nature a gate is subject to stresses from more factors than its weight, and the first place a gate will try to relieve its stress is on the hinges. Three hinges hang a gate far better than two. Err on the side of excess when you select the hinges and fasteners—make "heavy-duty" and "heavy-gauge" part of your selection criteria.

Fasteners

Most latches and hinges will come with their own fasteners, and most fasteners are woefully undersized. The screws may fit the holes, but they are not nearly long enough to hold the hinge securely. Screws should penetrate the wood frame as deeply as possible without going through the other side.

If the screws supplied with your hinges or latch aren't long enough to do the job, buy longer replacements of the same gauge. Using the same gauge will ensure that the screw fits snugly in the mounting hole and, in the case of hinges, sets flush with the hinge plate. Finding replacements for fasteners made to match the style of decorative hinges may be difficult. Sometimes an exact match isn't necessary. In this instance get the closest match you can.

Fasteners and hardware

Just as important as the quality of the lumber that goes into your fence is the quality of the fasteners that will hold it together. Whatever outdoor fasteners and hardware you choose, make sure they are rustproof—galvanized or stainless steel, brass, or other rust-resistant metal.

Nails

Once sold for so many pennies per hundred, nails today are sold by the pound. But nails still are described and sized by this old terminology—a 16-penny or a 4-penny nail. To further complicate things, "penny" is indicated by the letter d (probably for denarius, Latin for coin). What really matters is the length of the nail. In most cases the thickness of a nail follows its length.

Just as there are many sizes of nails, there are many types of nail shank. Each has a different holding power. Ringshank and spiral-shank nails grip the wood fibers better than smooth (common or box) nails and don't easily work their way out. In fact they can be difficult to remove.

Of all the sizes and shapes available, these nails work well for most fence projects:

Common or ringshank nails (16d) for the frame—in 2× or thicker stock.

Box or ringshank nails (8d or 10d) for the infill—in 1× or thinner stock.

Finishing nails (6d or 8d) for the fine trim.

Duplex nails for temporary fasteners; they have a double head that makes them easy to pull out when you strip away forms or braces for example.

For small jobs buy nails in 1-pound boxes or in bulk quantities by the pound. Keep an assortment of brads on hand. Brads look like miniature finishing nails; use them for molding and finishing jobs.

Screws

Screws hold better than nails and come in a multitude of styles. They're also easy to remove, which makes correcting mistakes easier. Your fence construction will require deck screws—usually in 2½- to 3½-inch lengths. Deck screws are coated to resist the elements and are sharp and self-sinking. You can drive them with a cordless drill about as quickly as you can drive nails.

Regardless of the size you use, predrill holes when driving them within 2 inches of the end of a board. This keeps the wood from splitting. Use a drill bit the same size as the screw shank (not the threads).

Screw heads vary in style and slot type. You need phillips, square-drive, or combination heads. Get square-drive heads if possible. They tend to strip out less than phillips-head screws.

A lag screw is a large screw with a hexagonal head used to secure heavy framing members and hardware. Tighten them with a wrench.

Bolts and brackets

Bolts, nuts, and washers provide a solid connection with excellent load-bearing strength. Use only zinc-coated or stainless-steel ones. Drill holes with a bit of the same diameter as the bolt shank. Bolts are sized by diameter, threads per inch, and length. For example, a ½-13×3-inch bolt is ½ inch in diameter, has 13 threads per inch, and is 3 inches long.

Metal fence brackets work well for quick installations and solid connections. Brackets can join rails to posts, prefabricated fence bays to posts, and louvered boards to posts (horizontal louvers) or rails (vertical louvers).

NAILS AND SCREWS

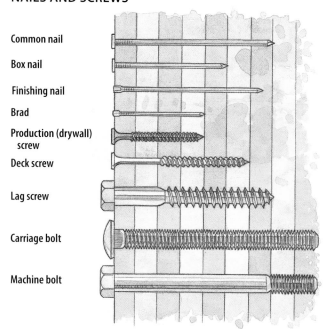

Common nail
Box nail
Finishing nail
Brad
Production (drywall) screw
Deck screw
Lag screw
Carriage bolt
Machine bolt

METAL FENCE BRACKETS

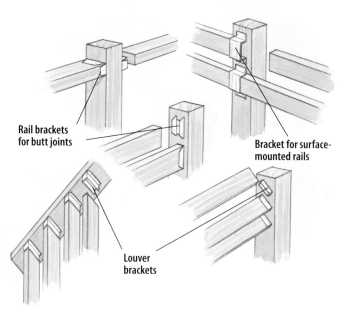

Rail brackets for butt joints

Bracket for surface-mounted rails

Louver brackets

BASIC BUILDING TECHNIQUES

Measuring and marking

Even the simplest fence will require a variety of measuring tools. You will probably use your tape measure most often. Get into the habit of starting work by clipping a steel tape to your belt.

There's an old carpenter's adage that says "measure twice, cut once." It's been around for years with good reason—it's amazingly easy to misread a measurement, even if you're a pro. Don't take anything for granted when measuring; mistakes waste time and material.

You'll need a sharp-pointed pencil to make accurate marks on your material. Carpenter's pencils, which have flat rather than round leads, work well for marking wood. For more accuracy use an awl, which looks like a short ice pick, or a scriber, which resembles a long steel toothpick.

Although you may make most rip cuts with a tablesaw, if you use a circular saw, equip it with a rip-cutting guide and make sure the guide does not wander off the edge of the board.

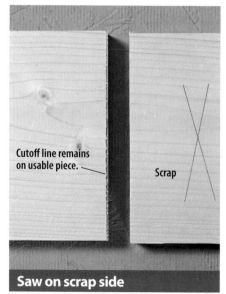

Cutoff line remains on usable piece.

Scrap

Saw on scrap side

Saw on the scrap side of the cutoff line, not straight down the middle of it. Otherwise your board will be half a saw kerf shorter than the length you want. Even this small discrepancy—typically 1/16 inch—can make a big difference.

Mark and cut board square.

Squaring up stock

Before you measure or fasten any board, make sure its end is square. Check it with a try square, layout square, or combination square, as shown. If it isn't square, mark the end and cut it square with a circular saw or mitersaw.

Marking crosscuts

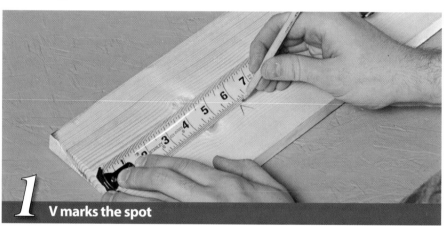

1 V marks the spot

Mark with a V. A dot is difficult to see, and a line almost always veers from the mark. Double-check your measurement before making any cuts. If you read the tape upside down, it is easy to mark at 5⅞ instead of 6⅛ inches, for instance.

2 Line up the square

Place the pencil point on the mark, then slide the blade of the square up to it. Draw the cutting line across the board. Mark the board on the waste side of the line with an X or some other sign to remind you which side to cut on.

Using squares and levels

Square refers to an exact 90-degree angle between two surfaces. When a material is level, it's perfectly horizontal; when it's plumb it's truly vertical.

Never assume that existing construction is square, level, or plumb. It probably isn't. To prove this to yourself, lay a level horizontally along any floor in your home, hold a level vertically against a wall section in a corner, or place a square on a door or window frame. Don't be alarmed at the results. Variation is normal because houses and other structures settle slightly on their foundations, throwing off square, level, and plumb.

How can you check a level's accuracy? Lay it on a horizontal surface and shim it, if necessary, to get a level reading. Then turn the level end for end. If you don't get the same reading, the level needs to be adjusted or replaced. Some models allow you to calibrate the level by rotating the glass vials. Laser levels come with instructions for their calibration.

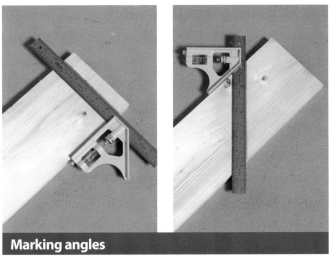

Marking angles

Use a combination square, layout square, or T-bevel to mark angles. A combination square and layout square can make only 45- and 90-degree angles. A T-bevel allows you to duplicate any angle and transfer it to the surface you're cutting.

Using a framing square

For large squaring jobs use a framing square, setting it on the inside or outside of the corner as the framing allows.

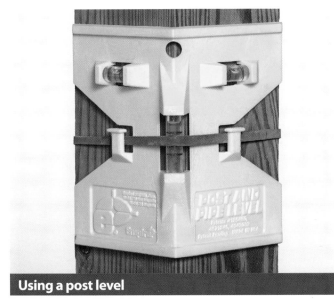

Using a post level

Fence posts must be plumb in two vertical planes, and a post level is made specifically for this job. Strap the level about halfway up the final length of the post. Adjust the post until all three bubbles are centered in their vials.

Plumb

Level

Using a carpenter's level

The longer the level the more precise your alignments will be. Use a 4-foot carpenter's level unless you don't have room. Use the end vials to plumb a board, the center vial to check for level.

Using a circular saw

Most circular saws come with a combination blade that will make crosscuts and rip cuts equally well.

If yours is equipped with a standard steel blade, replace it with a carbide-tooth combination blade. To change the blade on your saw, unplug it and retract the blade guard. Set the teeth of the blade firmly into the top of your outside work surface. Remove the bolt and tilt the blade out. Reverse the procedure to replace the blade.

Set the blade so it extends no more than ¼ inch (about 3 teeth) through the thickness of the stock. Release the saw plate latch to position the blade to the proper depth. For all cuts start the saw off the cut and push the blade into the board with a fairly rapid, constant forward motion.

Cutting lumber, especially pressure-treated stock, requires protection. Protect your eyes from flying chips and sawdust with safety glasses. If you are sensitive to pressure-treated lumber, use a face mask. When making frequent cuts wear ear protectors.

Cutting freehand

Freehand cuts will save you a lot of time, but they take practice. Set the edge of the board on a solid surface and hold the board at a 30- to 45-degree angle. Line up the saw guide with the cutline, start the saw, and let gravity pull it down the line. Keep the saw plate flat on the stock.

Crosscutting with a guide

With the saw plate flat on the board and the saw guide lined up with the waste side of the cutline, clamp a layout square against the edge of the saw plate. Start the saw and push it forward. With practice you can dispense with the clamp and hold the square with your other hand.

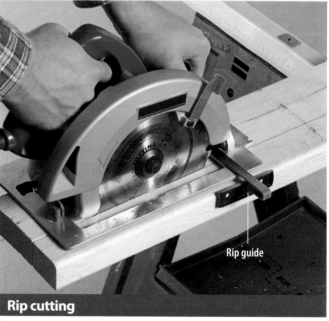

Rip guide

Rip cutting

Narrow rip cuts are easy to make with a rip guide. Line up the saw with the cutline and set the rip guide. Don't force the saw—the rip guide might flex off the line. For rip cuts not parallel to an edge, clamp a long straightedge to the board as a guide.

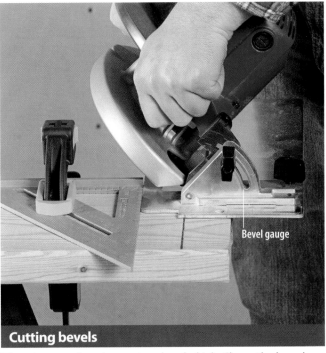

Cutting miters

You can cut miters freehand, but a layout square and a clamp will ensure a straight cut. Clamp the board to a solid surface. Retract the blade guard before starting the saw and don't push too hard. Cut the miter before you trim the length of the board; you can try again if you make a mistake.

Cutting bevels

Like miter cuts, bevels are a two-handed job. Clamp the board firmly to a work surface and clamp a layout square to the board so the blade will cut on the waste side of the line. Set the bevel gauge to the correct angle and check it with a protractor. Start the saw and ease it into the cut with a slow, constant speed.

Using a power mitersaw

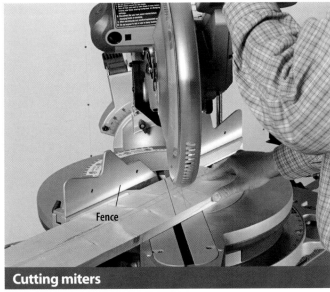

Cutting miters

Mark the cutline on the board and place the board against the fence. Position the board so the blade will cut about $1/16$ inch outside the cutline. Hold the board with one hand and squeeze the trigger with the other. Let the saw come to full speed and lower the blade into the work. Let the blade stop before raising the cutting head and removing the cut piece. Reposition the work and make successive cuts to the cutline.

Cutting bevels

To cut bevels set the miter scale at the angle of the cut and lock it. Then lock the blade at the angle of the bevel. Holding the board firmly against the fence, lower the blade and position the board directly under it. Then raise the saw, start the saw, and bring it to full speed. Lower the blade slowly and cut completely through the stock. Let the blade stop before raising the cutting head and removing the cut piece.

Fastening

It takes little time to master the basic skills associated with fastening wood. Here are some tips for driving nails and screws:

Using a hammer

For maximum leverage and control, hold the hammer near the end of the handle. Grasp the nail near its head and lightly tap it until it stands by itself. Keep your eye on the nail as you swing the hammer, letting the weight of the hammer do the driving. With the last hammer blow, set the head of the nail flush with the surface of the wood. The convex shape of the hammer face allows you to do this without marring the surface of the wood.

Using a cordless drill/driver

When driving screws with a cordless drill/driver, set the clutch so it disengages when the screw head is flush with the wood. To drive a screw hold it with one hand and give it a couple of turns with the drill until it sets itself in the wood. Keep the screwdriver tip square to the head and firmly in the recess. Start slowly with moderate pressure on the drill, increasing both the speed of the drill and the pressure until the screw is driven home. A pilot hole makes driving easier.

Driving nails

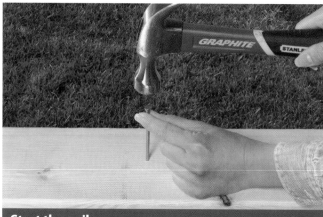

Start the nail

Hold the nail near its head. That way if you miss, the hammer will glance off your fingers rather than mash them. Start the nail with a light tap or two. Move your fingers when you no longer need to hold up the nail.

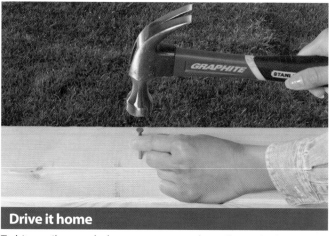

Drive it home

To hit a nail squarely, keep your eye on the nail, not the hammer. Let the weight of the hammer do the work. You don't need to apply a lot of muscle to it. After a while you'll find you can sink a nail in just three or four swings.

Avoid driving too far

Holding the nail at an angle or hitting it with a glancing blow of the hammer will cut the wood fibers as you drive the nail home. Overdriving the nail will create a pocket that will hold water.

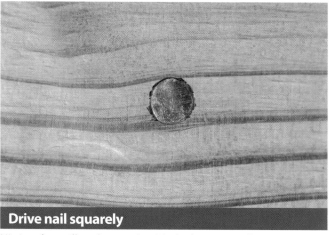

Drive nail squarely

Hitting the nailhead squarely with the hammer will avoid cut wood fibers. With the final hit of the hammer, set the nailhead so it just dents the surface.

Face-nailing

Skew nails for more hold

Skewed nails will increase their hold in the wood, especially when driven into end grain. Drive one nail at a 60-degree angle in one direction, then drive another nail in the opposite direction. Skewed nails make it difficult for the board to pull loose.

Stagger nails

Minimize splits, especially at the end of a board, by staggering the nails so they don't fall on the same grain lines. Drill pilot holes for the nails for added insurance against splits.

Make a scarf joint

When two framing members meet on top of a post, join them with a scarf joint centered on the post. Drive two fasteners on each side of the joint. A scarf joint adds visual interest and strength.

Nail rail twice

To fasten a through rail (one without a joint) to a post, drive two nails, offsetting them as shown. More nails won't make the joint stronger and could split the wood.

Toenailing

Blunt the point

Nailing near the end of a board tends to split the wood. To avoid this problem when toenailing, blunt the tip of the nail or drill a pilot hole first.

Start steep

To toenail a rail to a post, hold the nail at a steep angle, tap it once or twice, then lower the nail to about a 45-degree angle as you drive it home.

Fastening *(continued)*

Drilling pilot holes and driving screws

Deck screw, drill size in softwood
#4 screw, 1/16 inch
#6 screw, 3/32 inch
#8 screw, 7/64 inch
#10 screw, 1/8 inch
#12 screw, 9/64 inch
#14 screw, 5/32 inch

Drill a pilot hole

Driven too far

Driven correctly

Stop when head is flush

Drill a pilot hole of the correct size for the gauge of the screw into the joint at the angle of the fastener. Push the tip of the screw slightly into the hole and drive the screw, keeping the drill aligned with the screw and the bit firmly in the screw head. A magnetic screw finder bit helps hold the screw and drive it straight.

Overdriving a screw beyond the surface of the wood creates a pocket that can trap water. Use a cordless drill and set its clutch to release just when the screw is flush with the surface of the wood.

Counterboring

Spade bit same diameter as bolt washer

Bore 1/8" deeper than thickness of bolt head or nut.

Bore the big hole first

Twist drill bit same diameter as bolt shank

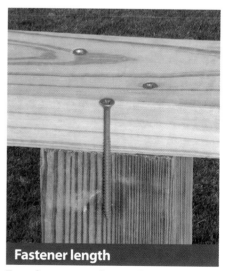

Fastener length

Lag screws and machine bolts look better with countersunk heads. To counterbore a hole start with a spade bit at least the same diameter as the washer under the head and large enough for a socket wrench to fit into the bore. Drill the counterbore 1/8 inch deeper than the thickness of the head or nut. Then using a twist drill bit the same diameter as the bolt, drill completely through the stock at the center of the counterbore. Slide the bolt through washers and use washers under the nut too. Caulk the recess with silicone to keep moisture out.

To make sure your fastened joints are strong and secure, use a fastener about three times as long as the thickness of the material you're fastening, unless it would go through the bottom piece.

Lag screws and bolts

Lag screws require a pilot hole three-fourths the diameter of the screw (a ³⁄₁₆-inch hole for a ¼-inch screw, for example). Bolts require a shank-size hole through the pieces joined.

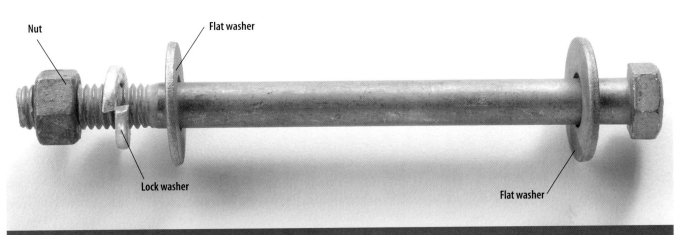

Nut   Flat washer   Lock washer   Flat washer

Machine bolt

Machine bolts have hexagonal heads and threads running partway or all the way along the shank. When fastening two pieces of wood together, slip a flat washer onto the bolt and slide the bolt through the holes in both pieces of material. Add another flat washer, then a lock washer. The flat washers keep the nut and the bolt head from digging into the wood. The lock washer prevents the nut from coming loose. Use two wrenches—one to hold the bolt and the other to draw the nut down onto the bolt.

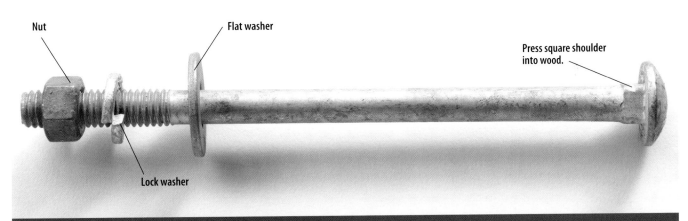

Nut   Flat washer   Press square shoulder into wood.   Lock washer

Carriage bolt

A carriage bolt has a plain, round head. Insert it into the hole and tap the bottom face of the head flush with the surface. No washer is needed under the head. The square or hexagonal shoulder under the head keeps the bolt from spinning as the nut is tightened.

Slip a flat washer, a lock washer, and a nut onto the bolt. Tighten the nut. The lock washer will keep the nut from working loose.

Cutting notches, mortises, and tenons

- ■ **TIME:** About 15 minutes to cut one notch; 30 minutes for mortise-and-tenon joint
- ■ **SKILLS:** Measuring and marking, sawing, using a chisel
- ■ **TOOLS:** Adjustable square or other square, circular saw, hammer, chisel, backsaw, clamps, drill, spade bit, mallet

Notches, mortises, and tenons increase the strength of fencing joints and enhance the aesthetic appeal of a fence design. If you haven't cut them before, you'll find the skill easy to acquire (take a few practice cuts on scrap). Make sure your cutting tools are sharp. Sharp tools are safer than dull tools and produce better looking—and better fitting—joints.

Although it's possible to cut these joints after setting the posts, it's a lot easier to cut them all at once before putting the posts into the postholes. This means that the joints must be at the same height from post to post or your fence will look crooked. Mark the position of the cuts precisely so they're the same from post to post, always measuring down from the top of the post to the joint. Then use the method illustrated on page 33 to bring the posts level with each other when setting them.

Notching posts

1 Lay out the notch

Using the width of your rails as the measurement, mark the top and bottom of the notch on the post with a combination square or layout square.

2 Saw between the marks

Set your circular saw to the depth of the notch (the thickness of the rail stock, commonly ¾ inch). Line up the side of the saw with the cutline and cut a series of kerfs about ¼ inch apart.

3 Clear out waste

Break the kerfed waste from the notch with a hammer, taking care not to mar the edge of the notch.

4 Chisel notch clean

Remove the waste with a wide, sharp chisel (bevel side down), clearing away the ridges until the bottom face of the notch is smooth and flat.

Cutting mortise-and-tenon joints

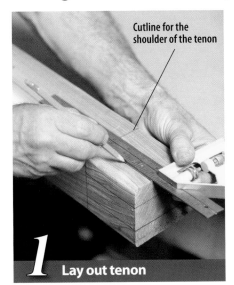

Cutline for the shoulder of the tenon

1 Lay out tenon

Mark the tenon's length (for a blind mortise, about $\frac{1}{16}$ inch shorter than the depth of the mortise) on all four sides of the stock, using a combination or layout square. In a through mortise the tenon should be $\frac{1}{8}$ inch longer than the thickness of the mortised stock.

2 Cut tenon sides

Clamp the tenon stock in a bench vise and, using a backsaw, carefully cut through the end of the stock to the shoulder line on all four sides. When you reach the shoulder line, make sure you saw perpendicular to the wood.

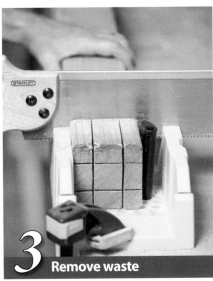

3 Remove waste

Clamp the tenon stock in a miter box and, using a backsaw, cut on the shoulder line to remove the waste. Repeat on the remaining sides.

Spade bit

4×4

Mortise outline

Scrap reduces tear-out if drilling through.

4 Drill mortise

Mortises, like notches, must be cut on the same plane on each post. Measure down from the top of each post so all the mortises begin at the same height. Then, using scrap or a cardboard template cut to the same size as the finished tenon, mark the outline of the mortise on the surface of the post. Using a spade bit about the same diameter as the width of the mortise, drill overlapping holes to remove most of the waste.

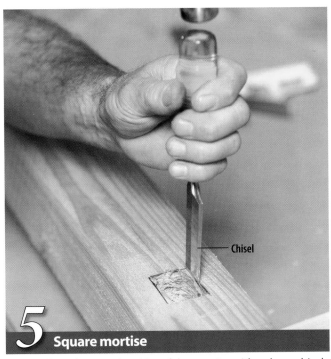

Chisel

5 Square mortise

After drilling clean up the sides of the mortise with a sharp chisel. Tap gently with a mallet. Smooth the surface with the flat side of the chisel. Be particular about the mortise corners; they must be smooth and square. For a through mortise turn the workpiece over and use the chisel to clean up the other side too.

Laying out a fence and setting posts

- **TIME:** About 8 hours, depending on length of fence and number of posts
- **SKILLS:** Measuring, marking, carpentry
- **TOOLS:** Circular saw, drill/driver, small sledge, mason's line, plumb bob, tripod, posthole digger, wheelbarrow, shovel, hammer, level, concrete hoe, tamper

Laying out a fence line is the first, and perhaps the most critical, step in constructing a fence. Do this correctly and the rest of your construction will proceed smoothly.

The illustrations on these pages show the essential steps in locating and lining up your posts. Before you start check with the city or county zoning office to make sure your project will comply with building codes and ordinances regarding setback from your property line. Most locations have a single phone number you can call to have the buried pipes and wires on your property located and marked before you dig. Your local electric utility may provide the number. If you can't find the number, call the North American One-Call Referral System at 888/258-0808.

1 Set up batterboards

Build batterboards from 2×4s by fastening crosspieces to the legs and driving them into the ground 3 to 4 feet beyond the ends of your fence line. Drive another pair of batterboards perpendicular to the first pair and parallel to the house, property line, or whatever plane in your landscape you will use to locate the fence. Tie mason's line to each pair of batterboards, pulling the line tight.

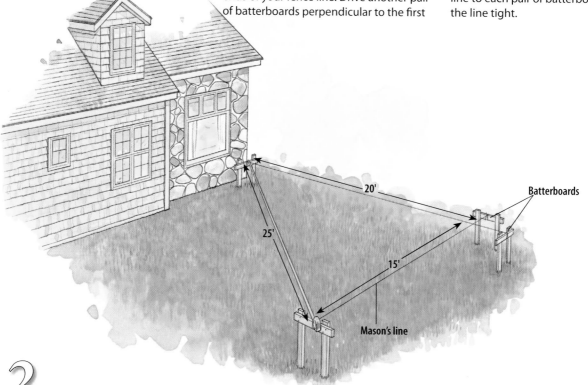

20'

25'

15'

Batterboards

Mason's line

2 Square corner

Starting at the intersection of the lines, measure 3 feet (or a multiple of three) out on one line and mark that point with a piece of tape. Measure 4 feet (or the same multiple) on the other line and mark it. Measure the distance between the pieces of tape. If the diagonal measures 5 feet (or the multiple), the corner is square. If necessary, adjust the lines until they make a 5-foot diagonal. Mark the final position of the lines on the crosspieces.

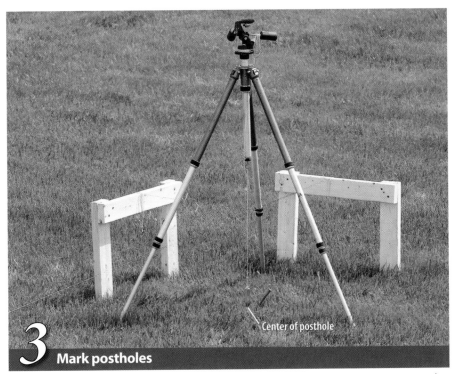

Center of posthole

3 Mark postholes

At each intersection drop a plumb bob to mark the location of the center of the post. Drive a stake or landscaping nail where the plumb bob comes to rest. Then move the plumb bob down the fence line to your next post location and mark its center with the same technique. Continue staking the post centers until you have marked all of them.

4 Dig postholes

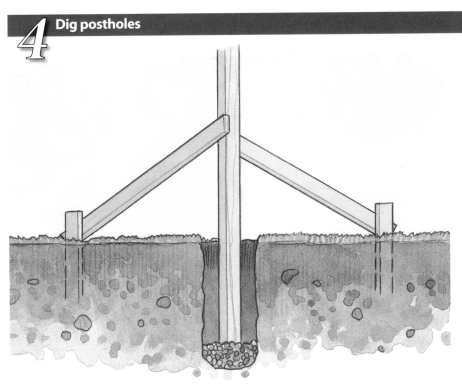

Remove the mason's lines from the batterboards (to get them out of your way). Then dig the postholes and shovel 3 inches of gravel into each one. The gravel lets water drain away from the bottom of the post and reduces the opportunities for rot. Set the post on the gravel and support it with temporary braces.

Laying out a fence and setting posts *(continued)*

In general, and in most areas of the country, posts anchored in concrete are the best way to support a fence or gate. However, in frost-free regions and in some soils, you can set the posts in a tamped earth-and-gravel base. Local building codes may have advice or standards about setting posts so check with your building department before digging the holes.

Define each corner with a pair of batterboards. For each batterboard make a pair of stakes by cutting a point on one end of two 2×4s. Attach a crossbar (see Step 1 on page 42) and drive the batterboards into the ground 3 to 4 feet outside the planned corner location. Locate them so that a line connecting the posthole centerlines will be at about the center of the crossbar.

However you decide to set your posts, be sure to dig holes for them 6 inches deeper than the frost line in your area to counter the effects of frost heave. Dig an 8-inch-diameter hole for each 4×4 post using a power auger, hand auger, or posthole digger (see pages 22–23). A 6×6 post requires a 10-inch-diameter hole.

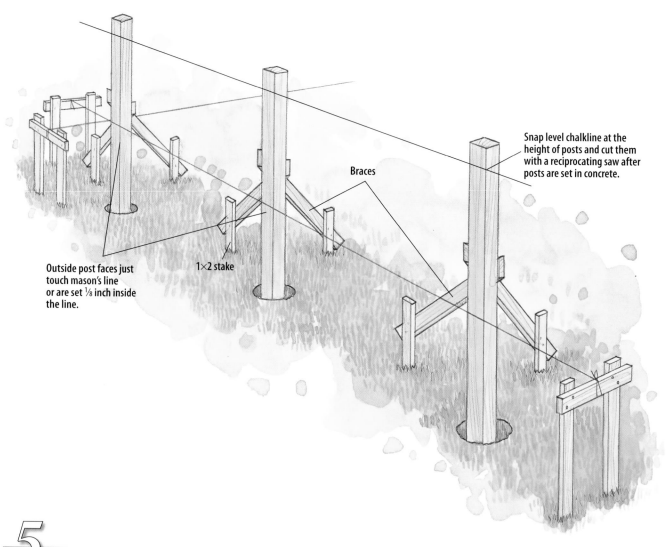

Braces

Snap level chalkline at the height of posts and cut them with a reciprocating saw after posts are set in concrete.

Outside post faces just touch mason's line or are set 1/8 inch inside the line.

1×2 stake

5 Plumb and align posts

Replace the mason's line on the batterboards, placing it outside the original marks by one-half the thickness of the post (1¾ inches for 4×4 posts). This will position the line at the outside face of the posts. Working on one post at a time with a helper, loosen the temporary braces and plumb each post with its outside face against the line. You can set the posts 1/8 inch inside the line to avoid moving the line with the posts. Attach braces to hold the posts in position.

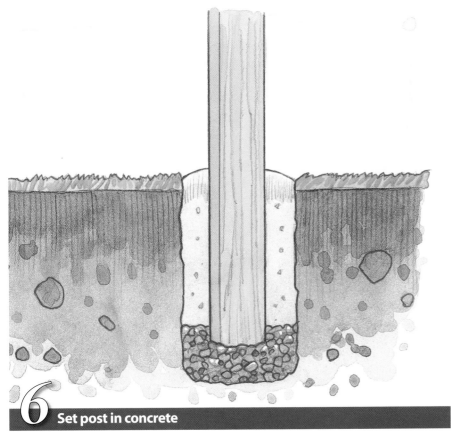

6 Set post in concrete

Add about 2 inches more gravel around the post. Mix and pour in concrete, tamping it as you fill to remove air bubbles. Slope the concrete around the top of the hole to drain away water that might cause rot. After the concrete sets remove the braces.

7 Caulk bottom of post

For a watertight seal around posts in concrete, apply silicone caulk around the post base after the concrete cures. That way, even if a post shrinks a bit over time, it will be protected against rot.

Concrete choices

Unless you are constructing an extremely long fence, consider using premixed bags of concrete that come with the correct amount of sand and gravel added to the cement; all you do is add water and mix. Premixed bags also make it easier for you to set some of the posts one day and come back the next day to set the rest of them without having your work schedule dictated by unused concrete.

You can also buy the cement in bags, order sand and gravel, and mix the concrete yourself. Mixing it yourself is less expensive but is more work. The convenience of premixed concrete is usually worth the extra money. In either case you will need gravel for the bottom of the postholes.

Mixing concrete

For most post-setting projects, mix three parts gravel with two parts sand and one part cement. If you mix your own concrete, move the mixing container as close to your posts as possible so you won't have to haul concrete across the yard in a wheelbarrow.

The amount of water needed depends on how wet the sand is. You'll need less water with wet sand than with dry sand. Test the wetness by squeezing some sand in your hand. If water seeps out, you'll need to add less water to the mix. If the ball compacts like moist clay, the mix will take more water.
As you mix the concrete, add very small amounts of water at a time. When the mix becomes one color—medium gray—and sticks slightly to a shovel held almost at 90 degrees, it's ready.

Once the concrete has cured, mark the height of the posts and cut them with a reciprocating saw (see illustration, opposite).

Laying out a fence and setting posts *(continued)*

Although setting posts in concrete is the most common method of anchoring them, there are a couple of alternatives. In some localities you can dig the holes and set the posts in tamped earth and gravel. And with a drive-in post anchor like the one shown (below right) you don't have to dig holes.

Setting posts in tamped earth and gravel

As with posts set in concrete, dig holes deep enough to go 6 inches below the frost line, then place several inches of gravel in the bottom of the holes. Posts in shallow holes or without the gravel can easily be knocked out of plumb.

Set a post in place, plumb it, and brace it with diagonal braces as shown on page 43. Then shovel about 4 inches of soil into the hole on all sides of the post and tamp it firmly. (A length of 2×4 makes a good tamper.) Follow this layer with a 4-inch layer of tamped gravel, alternating the earth and gravel until you've filled the hole. Then mound and tamp the soil around the base of the post; sloping the soil lets water drain away from the post and minimizes chances for rot. After several rainfalls check the slope. If the soil has settled, rebuild it and firmly compact it.

Anchoring posts to a patio or deck

If you're building a fence along the edge of a patio, deck, or porch, metal post bases will provide you with a handy answer to the question, "How do I anchor them?" Some post bases are made to be embedded in wet concrete. Others fasten to bolts in new or existing concrete. Some of these are adjustable and raise the bottom of the post about 1 inch off the concrete, which keeps the foot of the post above ground moisture and puddled water, reducing the risk of rot.

To install a bolt in existing concrete, drill a hole in the concrete, then inject epoxy cement into the hole with a syringe that comes with the epoxy. Set the bolt so that the end extends about ¾ inch above the surface.

After the epoxy cures, secure the base with a nut and washer. Then position the post in the base and nail or screw it in place.

You can also use metal anchors to join posts to another wooden structure such as a deck or porch. Just nail or screw the base to the surface. A simple U-shape base will work where no moisture protection is necessary.

Anchor answers

When building and anchoring a structure, keep these points in mind:

- Check local building codes for specific requirements.
- Don't build a fence on an existing patio or deck without attaching one end to the house, permanent structure, or post embedded in the ground. Ideally a deck or patio fence should be anchored at both ends.
- Always use the fasteners specified for the base.

Setting posts in tamped earth and gravel

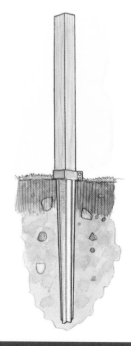

Set posts in soil

To set posts in soil, lay a gravel base, then shovel soil into the hole, filling it partially. Tamp the soil fill to compact the earth firmly around the post. Alternate layers of soil with layers of gravel, tamping every layer for a solid fill.

Spike post base

A spike post base drives into the ground without digging. The length of the spike depends on the height of the fence. Make sure local codes allow this kind of base for your fence posts.

Laying out a curved fence line

- **TIME:** About 1 hour to lay out a curve
- **SKILLS:** Measuring and marking
- **TOOLS:** Small sledge or hammer, length of rebar for scriber, mason's line

Curved fences increase the attractiveness of a fence line and can solve some tricky layout problems. They can skirt trees, large rocks, and other obstructions. Round corners can help a fenced area seem less cramped.

Curved fences have some structural limitations, however. They're difficult to construct between post spans shorter than 4 feet or longer than 6 feet, they need at least three posts, and the infill has to be narrow, especially in tight curves. Even if you draw the curve precisely on your final plan, you may need to change it to fit the realities of the actual location.

When you set the posts, note their orientation; for most infill styles the post faces should fall on the arc line.

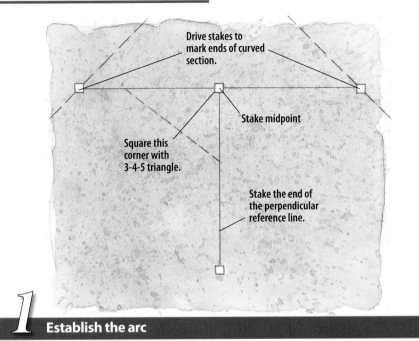

Drive stakes to mark ends of curved section.

Stake midpoint

Square this corner with 3-4-5 triangle.

Stake the end of the perpendicular reference line.

1 Establish the arc

Begin your layout by driving stakes at both ends of the curve. Then tie a tight line between them. Drive a stake at the midpoint of that line and extend a perpendicular line to a stake that will serve as the end of your "compass line."

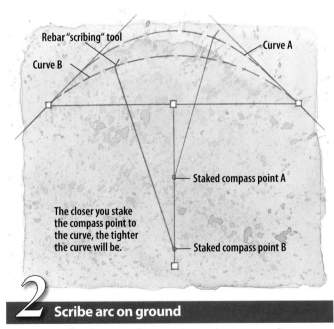

Rebar "scribing" tool

Curve A

Curve B

Staked compass point A

The closer you stake the compass point to the curve, the tighter the curve will be.

Staked compass point B

2 Scribe arc on ground

Drive a pipe, landscape spike, or stake on the compass line at the point where you want to center the curve. Note that the placement of this "compass point" will determine the depth of the arc and the radius of the curve. Loop one end of a length of mason's line around the center point and tie a short piece of ½-inch rebar to the other end. Scribe the arc of your curve in the ground with the rebar.

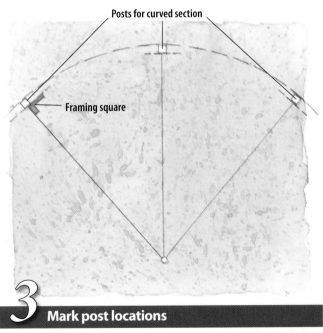

Posts for curved section

Framing square

3 Mark post locations

Mark each post location on the arc you scribed and dig the holes. Set the posts in each hole and brace them. Run the mason's line from the compass point to the post and use a framing square to make sure the post is perpendicular to the line.

Laying out sloped fences

Fencing a slope calls for some modification of the basic layout techniques shown earlier in this chapter. Essentially you have two options—contoured fencing or stepped fencing.

Contoured fencing is easier to install, especially on irregular or rolling slopes. The rails of a contoured frame run parallel to the slope and to each other, and the infill is cut to follow the slope. Rail fences and fences with surface-mounted infill make good contour models. Inset infill does not work well with this type.

Stepped fencing resembles a stairway—its rails run horizontally and parallel to each other, and each bay steps down the slope by an equal or unequal amount, depending on how you want the design to look. Stepped fences are more difficult to plan and install so they are better suited to straight slopes. Almost any board fence can be adapted to a stepped fence.

Marking postholes on a slope requires a different technique than marking them on level ground. If you mark the width of the bays on the sloped ground, the posts will end up closer together than you want them. To space the posts correctly, you must mark them from a level line.

To establish a level line, drive a stake at each end of the slope where the end posts will be. Make the lower stake tall enough to be level with the top of the grade. Tie mason's line tightly between the stakes. On short slopes tie the upper end at grade level and slip a line level on it. On long slopes tie the line about a foot above grade so you'll have room to use a water level to level the line at the lower stake. Mark the line with tape at intervals equal to your bay width and drop a plumb bob from each mark to locate the postholes.

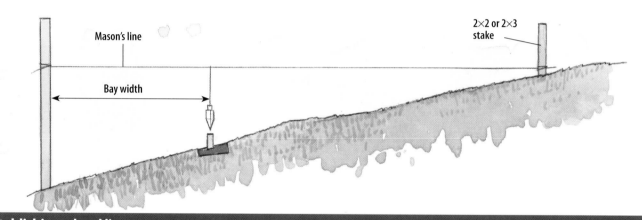

Mason's line

Bay width

2×2 or 2×3 stake

Establishing a level line

Stepped fencing starts by staking out a level line across the slope. Mark the line with tape at intervals equal to the width of the bays.

Mark posthole locations by dropping a plumb bob from the marks on the level line.

Staking a contoured layout

To stake out a contoured fence, establish a level line and mark the posthole locations. Then take down the stakes from the level line and drive batterboards at both the top and bottom of the slope and at every change in grade. Tie mason's line between them.

Adjust the position of the line so it follows the fence line along its length. Adjust any posthole markers that don't fall directly under the mason's line.

TYPICAL STEPPED FRAMEWORK

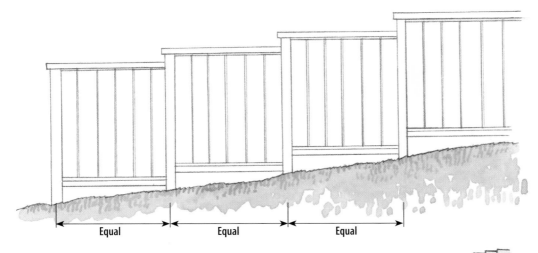

Equal   Equal   Equal

TYPICAL CONTOURED FRAMEWORK

Equal   Equal   Equal

Two ways to climb a hill

A fence can either step up a slope with a stepped framework or follow the slope with a contoured framework. The infill style is often the determining factor; inset infill such as louvers or basket weave is best suited to a stepped framework. A board fence could be built in either style.

Staking a stepped layout

To stake out a stepped fence, establish a level line and mark post locations as described. Set each post in concrete, leaving the posts taller than their final length. Let the concrete cure.

Measure the exact rise and run of the slope and determine the step-down distance for each bay.

Mark the step-down—measuring from the top—on the uppermost post. With a water level, mark the next post at that height. Cut that post to height, mark the step-down on it, and repeat for the next post. Repeat for all of the posts.

Step-down

Rail

Toenail here

Water level

Cutline

Layout line

Building an edge-rail fence frame

- **TIME:** With posts set, about 15 minutes to cut and attach two rails in one fence bay
- **SKILLS:** Measuring and marking, cutting, fastening
- **TOOLS:** Tape measure, chalkline, circular saw, drill/driver, hammer, level

Almost all fence designs rely on one of two rail styles—edge rails or flat rails. Edge rails are installed with the widest of their faces perpendicular to the ground. That means they resist sagging more effectively than flat rails. This positioning also allows you more choices when it comes to mounting the infill although most kinds of inset infill require flat rails, not edge rails.

Where you position the rails is largely a matter of design choice, but the rail position will affect the kind of infill and the method you use for hanging it. Some designs call for the rails to be set flush with the posts along the entire length of the fence. Others require flush rails that alternate from one side of the posts to the other on every other bay. Other designs look better with the rails mounted on the surface of the posts, centered between them, or mounted in notches.

One of the primary decisions you'll need to make is which side of the fence will be the neighbor's—and whether it matters. Certain fence designs are clearly one-sided. Even though the fence you're building is your fence and it's on your property or property line, legal ownership will not necessarily prevent hard feelings if the neighbors must look at the backside of it.

Such neighborly disagreements can be acrimonious but can often be avoided by constructing friendly fences—designs that look good from both sides.

It can also help to give the neighbors some warning that you're going to build a fence. Showing them a friendly design will allay some of their fears and indicate to them that you respect their feelings. The fence might be yours, but the view is community property.

Whatever the position of the rails, use the techniques illustrated to install them.

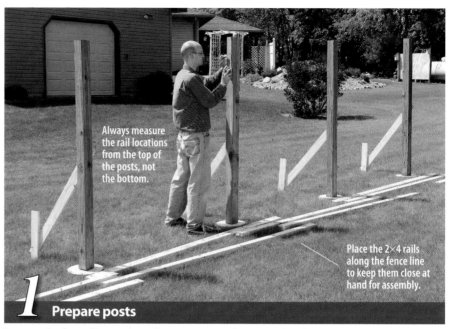

Always measure the rail locations from the top of the posts, not the bottom.

Place the 2×4 rails along the fence line to keep them close at hand for assembly.

1 Prepare posts

Lay out the fence line and set the posts in concrete. Let the concrete cure and leave the braces up—they add stability when you're driving fasteners. Cut the posts to the correct height and measure down from the top of each post to mark the location of the top and bottom rails. For fences on level ground, you can mark the end posts and snap a chalkline to mark the intermediate posts. For stepped or contoured frames, you'll have to measure and mark each pair of posts separately. Distribute the rails along the fence line so they will be handy.

Usually 6"

Support one end of the rail with scrap wood.

Bottom rail 3" to 6" above the ground

2 Cut rail to length

Mark each rail for cutting by measuring the distance between posts or by holding the uncut rail in place and marking it as shown here. Don't cut all the rails at once—the space between each pair of posts may vary a fraction of an inch, and rails that are even ⅛ inch short won't reach. Always saw just to the outside of your mark to make your rail fit snugly.

3 Attach rail

Predrill the holes for fasteners and toenail the top rails to the posts with 10d nails, 3½-inch galvanized or treated screws, or rail hangers. Then attach the bottom rails. When the frame is complete, remove the braces if you have not done so already.

Line up centered rails

If rails will be centered inside the post faces, mark the center of the posts and the rails after you cut them. When you attach the rails, line up the marks with each other.

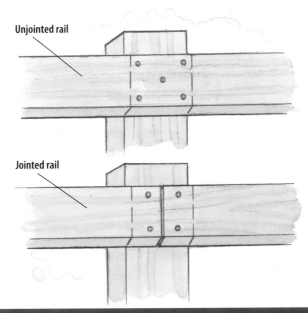

Unjointed rail

Jointed rail

Surface rails

If edge-mounted rails will be fastened to the outside faces of the posts, use one of the nailing patterns above, depending on whether the rails are jointed or unjointed.

51

Building a flat-rail frame

- **TIME:** About 1 hour to install rails and kickboards across three posts
- **SKILLS:** Measuring and marking, cutting, fastening
- **TOOLS:** Tape measure, chalkline, circular saw, drill/driver, hammer, level

Flat-rail designs are suited to surface-mounted and inset infill. In both cases the rails are fastened with their narrow edges flush with the faces of the posts. For surface-mounted infill this provides a surface on which to fasten the boards between the frames. For inset infill the wide faces of the rails provide plenty of space to attach the infill and the stops or nailers that hold them in place.

Although building a flat-rail frame involves essentially the same techniques as building edge-rail framing, a few details need additional attention:

- Because one of the functions of the top rail is to tie the posts together in a single structural unit and because joints reduce the top rail's strength, you should minimize the number of joints. For rail stock get the longest boards possible. On a short fence a board that will span the entire length of the fence is ideal. On long fences always use top-rail stock long enough to span at least three posts.
- Always butt top rails on the center of a post. This adds strength to the joint and gives you a surface wide enough for your fasteners. The same goes for cap-rail stock. If you're installing a cap rail, you can attach it at any time in the process of building the frame (but after fastening the top rail).
- Consider adding a cap rail to the fence design (illustration on opposite page, above right). This second top rail gives the fence a finished look and adds strength to the frame. Combined with a kickboard (opposite page), this can minimize fence sagging.

LOOKS MATTER

Posts and rails contribute to the overall look of the fence in a flat-frame fence with inset infill. If the fence will be painted, pressure-treated posts and rails work well. But if you are installing inset cedar or redwood infill that will be stained or left natural, you will probably be happier with posts and rails of the same lumber.

Distribute the rails along the fence line so they will be handy.

1 Prepare posts

Lay out the fence line and set the posts in concrete. Let the concrete cure and leave the braces up—they add stability. Cut the posts to the correct height and measure down from the top of each post to mark the location of the bottom rails.

For fences on level ground, you can mark the end posts and snap a chalkline to mark the intermediate posts. For stepped or contoured frames, you'll have to measure and mark each pair of posts separately.

2 Attach rails and kickboards

Use the longest top-rail stock possible to reduce the number of joints. Cut the top-rail sections so any joints will be centered on the top of the posts. Drill pilot holes in the top-rail sections and fasten them to the posts with 10d nails or 3½-inch rustproof screws. Measure, cut, and attach the cap rail, bottom rails, and kickboards.

Although flat rails are by nature more prone to sag than edge rails, there are a couple of things you can do to shore them up. A kickboard mounted under the bottom of the lower rail and toenailed at both ends to the posts will add strength to the bay and help keep the whole assembly from sagging under its own weight. Adding one or two additional rails within the bay will also minimize sagging.

Because you might find it difficult to set a kickboard in the space between the bottom rail and the ground after the rail is fastened, screw the kickboard to the bottom of the rail first and then toenail the assembled pieces between the posts.

As with edge rails, you can set flat rails at various heights from the ground and in dadoes cut in the interior faces of the posts. Varying the height of dadoed rails from bay to bay can add style to the backside of the fence.

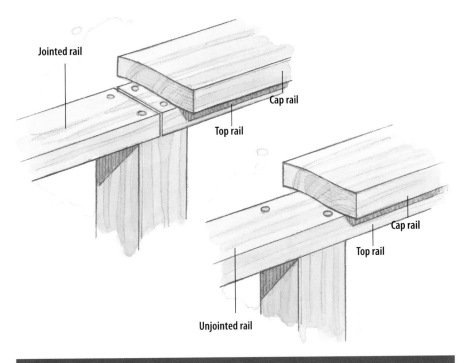

Jointed rail

Cap rail

Top rail

Cap rail

Top rail

Unjointed rail

Fastening the top rail

How you drive the top-rail fasteners will depend on whether the rail is unjointed or jointed. Use the pattern above appropriate to your installation. Fasten the cap rail with the same pattern, but do not install a cap-rail joint over a top-rail joint. Offset cap-rail joints by at least one post.

Installing a kickboard

Kickboards close the gap under the bottom rail, add a decorative touch to your fence, and keep animals from crawling under it. They also help keep flat rails from sagging. You can attach them to the faces of the posts or inset them under the bottom rail. It's usually easier to install an inset kickboard on the bottom rail and toenail the entire assembly to the posts. Grooving the bottom rail to accept the kickboard is an option. Fasten the kickboard to the bottom of the rail with 3-inch screws every 8 to 10 inches. Toenail it to the posts at the ends. Trim your kickboard with a 1×2 if you want. Make the kickboard from pressure-treated lumber or the heartwood of a decay-resistant species such as cedar or cypress because the board touches the earth and is subject to rot.

SURFACE-MOUNTED KICKBOARD

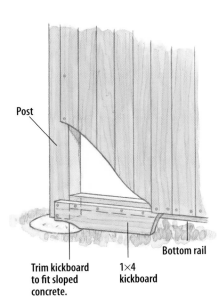

Post

Bottom rail

Trim kickboard to fit sloped concrete.

1×4 kickboard

INSET KICKBOARD

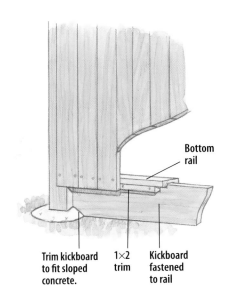

Bottom rail

Trim kickboard to fit sloped concrete.

1×2 trim

Kickboard fastened to rail

Installing surface-mounted infill

■ **TIME:** Less than 1 hour to attach and trim board infill in an 8-foot bay; time varies depending on infill type and style
■ **SKILLS:** Measuring and marking, cutting, fastening
■ **TOOLS:** Tape measure, circular saw, hammer, drill/driver, level, chalkline

Of all the aspects of fence construction, installing the infill is probably the most enjoyable because you can begin to see the results of your planning and layout. It's at this step that the structure you've been toiling over begins to look like a fence. The tasks associated with hanging the infill are repetitive—you'll fall into a rhythm and the work will go quickly.

Surface-mounted infill requires less measuring and fitting than inset infill so fences built this way go up quickly. You don't even need to precut boards to length for surface-mounted infill when fencing on level ground; you can let the boards run wild—at random heights—and then cut them to a finished line all at once. Infill boards finished with a cut top—pickets, points, or dog ears, for example—must be cut to size before you put them up. If the infill is spaced, like pickets, make a jig to ensure consistent spacing (see page 58). A board ripped to the correct width is an easy way to gauge spacing.

Flat-rail frame or edge-rail frame with the rails flush with the posts

1 Prepare the frame

Build the fence frame and let the concrete set. Tack a 1×4 batten to the posts (spanning at least 3 bays) where you want the bottom of the infill. When you install the infill, set each board on the batten. This will keep the infill at a consistent height above the ground.

A surface-mounted classic
A picket fence is a classic example of surface-mounted infill. Pickets with alternating top styles make this fence attractive. For a design like this, pickets must be cut to length before installation.

Let top edge of infill run wild.

2 Attach infill

Distribute your infill materials along the fence line so they're close at hand. Begin fastening the infill at an end, corner, or gatepost. Attach 1× stock with 8d nails or 2-inch treated screws; hang thinner material with 6d nails or 1½-inch screws. Check the leading edge of the infill with a carpenter's level every 3 or 4 feet to make sure it is plumb.

It is tricky to get the bottom of each board lined up with the adjacent one. Tack a batten along the bottom of the posts—spanning at least three posts—and this task becomes a snap. The batten allows you to set each infill board directly on it—it's like having a third hand. Level the batten if the ground is level; let it follow the slope for a contoured fence. Whether level or sloped, keep the batten at the same distance from the ground along its length by measuring and marking its location from the top of the posts. Don't try to eyeball the clearance between the ground and the batten—

it's almost impossible to get it right without measuring.

- If your fasteners are less than 2 inches from the ends of the infill boards, predrill holes to keep the infill from splitting. Fasteners 2 inches or more from the ends of the infill are less likely to split the wood, but it's still wise to drill pilot holes.
- If the infill goes out of plumb, remove it and correct the problem—it's easier in the long run to fix a mistake early than to try adjusting subsequent boards.
- Mark the height of your infill on both ends of the bay, snap a chalkline

between the marks, and trim the infill along the line. To cut it quickly and accurately with a circular saw, measure down from the chalkline a distance equal to the distance from your circular saw's blade to the edge of its soleplate. Watch out for uneven joints; they will catch the saw.

- If you will be staining or painting the fence, prepare the surfaces according to the finish manufacturer's instructions and apply the finish. Protect your landscaping and plantings with plastic tarps.

Board tops are uneven until trimmed

Tack a batten to guide circular saw.

3 Trim top

Mark the finished height of the completed infill at both ends of the fence, tack a guide to the fence, and trim the infill with a circular saw.

Installing inset infill

- **TIME:** About 1 hour to install board infill in one 8-foot bay; time varies with other infill types and styles
- **SKILLS:** Measuring and marking, cutting, fastening
- **TOOLS:** Tape measure, chalkline, circular saw, hammer, level

Inset infill lends itself to many fence styles: this is the ideal way to install lattice panels as well as other types of panel fencing—plywood, acrylic, and tongue and groove. You'll also use it if you're building a basket weave or featherboard fence. With its 1× or 2× stops containing the infill boards and functioning as trim, it creates a stylish finished look for a variety of materials.

Inset infill requires careful marking of the position of the stops and more exacting construction, but it produces clean lines and shows an equally attractive face on both sides. It's the ideal construction if you're looking for a friendly fence that will appeal to your next-door neighbors.

Your planning should include careful computation of the total width of the infill boards and stops. Because a 2×4 rail is actually 3½ inches wide, you'll have to make sure of two things:
- That the combined width of the materials does not exceed the width of the rails.
- That the entire assembly, infill boards and stops together, is centered in the frame.

Add the width of the pieces together and subtract it from the width of the rails. Divide the remaining amount in half: This is the width of the reveal on each side, the space between the stop and the edge of the rail. The combined width of 1× infill and two 1× stops—2¼ inches—leaves 1¼ inches of rail exposed on a 3½-inch rail. Set your first stop ⅝ inch from the edge of the rails (half of 1¼ inches = ⅝ inch). Use a combination square set to ⅝ inch to mark each interior corner of the frame. Snap chalklines at these marks and nail the stops on the lines. Inset infill calls for a square fence frame, but you can usually work around minor flaws. Wide stops, for example, can hide gaps. And you can cut sheet materials to fit exactly.

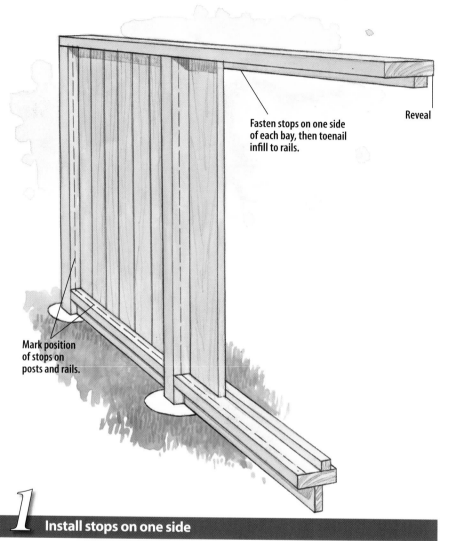

Fasten stops on one side of each bay, then toenail infill to rails.

Reveal

Mark position of stops on posts and rails.

1 Install stops on one side

Mark the position of the stops and snap guidelines on the posts and rails. Cut the stops and infill to length. Fasten the stops to one side of the bay opening with either 6d or 8d finishing nails depending on the thickness of the stops. Working from the open side, fit the infill into the frame. Toenail the infill to the rails not to the stops. Check for plumb as you go.

STOPS CAN BRING STYLE TO A FENCE

Square or rectangular stock makes solid, functional stops. For a different look or to enhance a particular infill style, install ordinary quarter-round molding or cove molding in ¾-inch size. Either would give board infill a more finished look. Use solid moldings, not finger-joint interior moldings. You also could plane or rout a chamfer on one edge of square or rectangular stock to make stops that stand out from the usual.

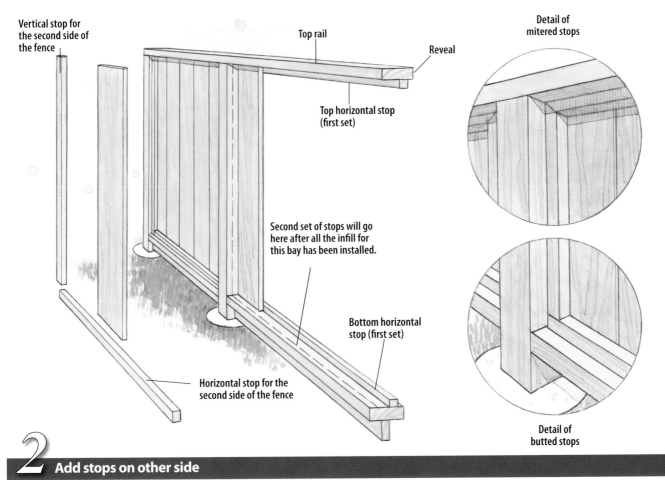

Vertical stop for the second side of the fence

Top rail

Reveal

Top horizontal stop (first set)

Detail of mitered stops

Second set of stops will go here after all the infill for this bay has been installed.

Bottom horizontal stop (first set)

Horizontal stop for the second side of the fence

Detail of butted stops

2 Add stops on other side

Continue attaching infill in the bay. If you need to trim the width of the infill to fit the frame, rip the last three boards narrower by a fraction of the total. That way your last board will not look noticeably narrower than the rest. Fasten the other set of stops to the frame.

BOARD ON BOARD WITH FLAT RAILS

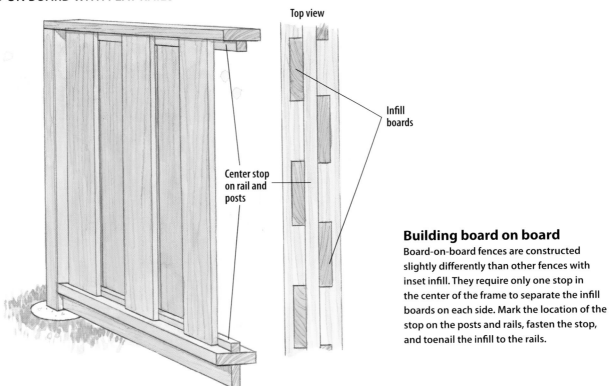

Top view

Infill boards

Center stop on rail and posts

Building board on board

Board-on-board fences are constructed slightly differently than other fences with inset infill. They require only one stop in the center of the frame to separate the infill boards on each side. Mark the location of the stop on the posts and rails, fasten the stop, and toenail the infill to the rails.

57

Infill installation tips

Following a few general tips will make any fence style more professional looking and longer lasting.

- Don't scrimp on fasteners—either in quality or quantity. Treated nails or deck screws cost slightly more but will last longer and stain the fence less than untreated fasteners. Galvanized fasteners are not immune from rust. Stainless-steel fasteners are the best choice.

- In addition to their own weight, fences have to carry the loads imposed by rain, snow, wind, and climbing kids. Much of this stress falls on the fasteners—use plenty of them.

- Hang boards plumb. Check the infill as you go—every few feet at least—with a 4-foot level (shorter levels won't be accurate). If the infill has gotten out of plumb, take your work apart and correct it. Out-of-plumb infill only gets worse.

- Make bottom edges flush and smooth. Use battens to help place the infill (tack a 1×3 or 1×4 to the surface of the posts) unless your design intentionally calls for random lengths. Reposition the batten as you work your way down the line.

- To finish a wild-top edge, snap a chalkline at the cutting height. Then tack a 1×3 or 1×4 guide so a circular saw's soleplate can ride on it. Set the blade deep enough to cut through the infill, but no deeper. Rest the saw on the cutting guide and cut the entire top of the fence in one pass.

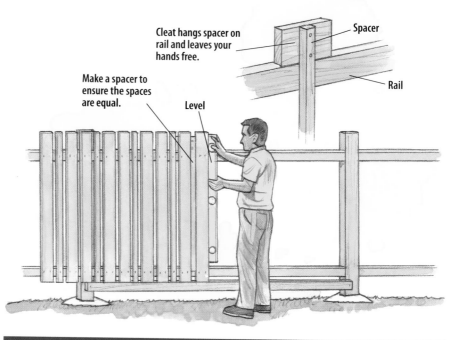

Spacing the infill

Equalize the spaces between infill boards with a cleated spacer. Hang the cleat on the top rail so you can free both hands to hold the infill as you fasten it. Check the infill for plumb every 3 or 4 feet.

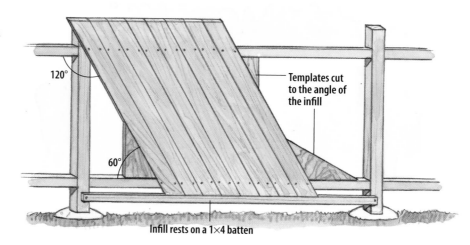

Cutting angled infill

Cut templates to properly position angled infill in the frame. Cut the bottom of the infill to the correct angle and set the boards on a level batten while you fasten them. Cut the top edge to length or let the tops of the boards run wild and trim them with a circular saw. Use another batten to guide the saw and keep the top edge straight.

Building curved fence sections

- **TIME:** 2 hours or longer for a corner
- **SKILLS:** Measuring and marking, cutting, fastening
- **TOOLS:** Tape measure, circular saw, drill/driver, hammer, chisel, bevel gauge, level

Building a curved fence section requires a careful layout (see page 47). Once you have scribed the arc on the ground, use the directions illustrated to locate and set the posts and install the rails—either curved or segmented. Hang the infill as you would on a straight rail.

You should construct your curved fence section in the same manner as the straight sections. For example, if you built the straight sections with flush-mounted rails, your curved section will have to follow suit. The best solution is to design the fence so the rails are notched into the posts. If your straight rails are face-mounted, your curved rails should be too.

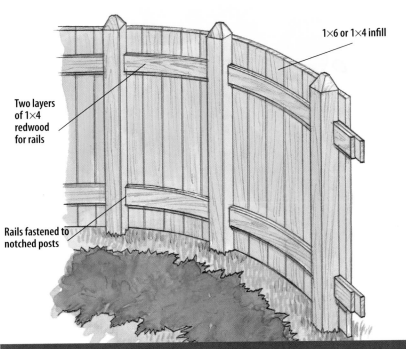

Two layers of 1×4 redwood for rails

Rails fastened to notched posts

1×6 or 1×4 infill

Continuous curve

Make the rails from layers of thin stock—four layers of ³⁄₈-inch redwood, two layers of 1×4 redwood with ¹⁄₄-inch saw kerfs spaced 1¹⁄₂ to 2 inches apart, or unkerfed 1×4 redwood for shallow bends. Soak the rails in water to make them more pliable.

Fasten the first rail layer on the posts (or into 3¹⁄₂×1¹⁄₂-inch notches) with 2-inch screws. Butt-join successive pieces at the center of a post. Cut the next layer so the joint won't fall on top of a joint in the first layer. Fasten this layer with screws long enough to go through both layers and into the post.

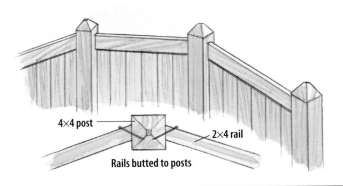

4×4 post

2×4 rail

Rails butted to posts

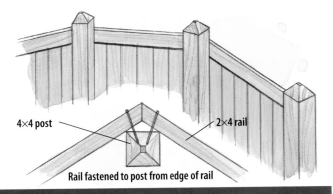

4×4 post

2×4 rail

Rail fastened to post from edge of rail

Segmented rails

For segmented rails start by determining the angle for the rail ends. Tack a level 2×4 to the outside edges of two posts. Hold a straightedge against the side face of one post and extend the line across the top of the 2×4. Cut the 2×4 at this angle and use it as a template to cut all the rails.

Cut the rails to fit between the posts for flush-mounted rails, as shown in the illustration at left. Install surface-mounted rails as shown in the illustration above.

Dealing with obstacles

When you're planning your fence and discover that your proposed fence line is going to pass through tree trunks, large rocks, or gullies and other depressions that you can't remove or eliminate, don't give up. You have more solutions than you might think. You can skirt some obstructions such as trees and freestanding boulders by building a semicircular or three-sided fence section around them. When you can't go around an obstacle, try these simple solutions.

It is usually not a good idea to nail fencing to the trunk of a tree. Puncture wounds and bark damage can expose a tree to disease and insect invasion and disturb the flow of water and nutrients. Digging postholes near a tree can damage the root system. Reposition the fence line or stop it short of the tree on either side as illustrated so the tree can continue to grow. Bring the fence as close to the tree as possible and support the extensions next to it with short posts under the bottom rail. Set these short posts on concrete post pads.

When a fence bridges a depression in the landscape, adjust the infill on the bottom to fill the gap. Conversely you can adjust the bottom rail position and trim the infill to clear mounds or other high obstructions.

OTHER INFILL

Some types of infill work better then others when avoiding obstacles. Surface-mounted board infill, as shown in the illustrations, adapts most easily to obstacles. If you want louvers, basket weave, or another inset infill for the fence but need to follow one of the examples in the lower two illustrations (right), extend or cut back the kickboard on the flat-rail frame to allow for the obstacle. In the rock example (right) you could position the rail higher and install a wider kickboard in the affected bay.

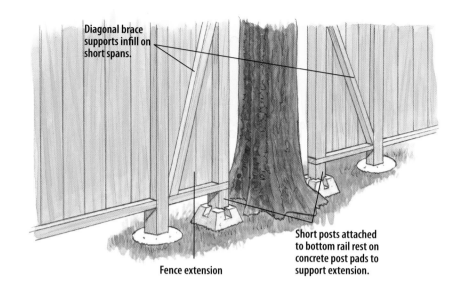

Diagonal brace supports infill on short spans.

Fence extension

Short posts attached to bottom rail rest on concrete post pads to support extension.

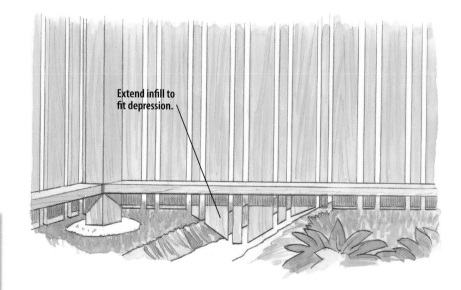

Extend infill to fit depression.

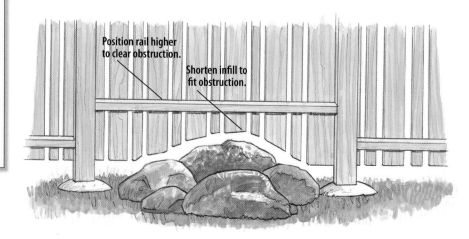

Position rail higher to clear obstruction.

Shorten infill to fit obstruction.

BUILDING FENCES

Vertical board fence

- **TIME:** Allow 2 or more days
- **SKILLS:** Site layout, digging, concrete work, measuring and marking, cutting, fastening
- **TOOLS:** Layout, digging, and concrete tools for layout and setting posts; carpentry tools for building fence

Vertical board fences are probably the most common style. That's because they are easy to build and you can vary their design almost infinitely. Styles with surface-mounted infill have front and back sides, so you'll have to decide whether you or the neighbors will see the frame. Installing inset infill makes a fence look the same from both sides.

A fence with no gaps between the boards can create a fully enclosed, very private space. It can also feel confining. You can relieve that by alternating the height of the bays or adding a lattice top panel to add variety and open up the view. Or you can alternate boards with slats—1×6s with 1×2s—and leave spaces between them. This design looks refined and adds an interesting play of light and shadow.

Whatever fence style you choose, first decide how wide you want the bays to be. Then divide that measurement by the width of the boards (or the boards and spaces) to choose the infill you want.

A vertical board fence usually reaches 6 feet. It can be taller, if necessary and if codes permit.

A basic board fence
Solid board fencing can provide complete privacy. This 6-foot fence is built with dog-eared boards to add a touch of style.

HOW TO USE VERTICAL BOARD FENCES

- Defining spaces: very good but can seem imposing
- Security: excellent, especially with heights of more than 6 feet
- Privacy: good; closed styles can provide considerable privacy
- Creating comfort zones: fair; it blocks sun but can force wind into gusty downdrafts

Fence boards
Fence boards are usually 1×6 or 1×8 lumber. Some dealers sell thinner stock in nominal 6- and 8-inch widths for fencing. Add interest and style by cutting the tops to a decorative shape.

SOLID BOARD FENCE

6"
2×4
5'–6' height
1×8
2×4
8"
4"

1 Assemble the frame

Lay out and set posts for 6- to 8-foot bays. Then build a flat-rail frame (page 52) or an edge-rail frame (page 50) with the rails flush with one face of the posts. On longer bays you may want to add a center rail to help keep the infill from sagging. Toenail the rails to the posts.

2 Cut the top pattern

Use 1×6 or 1×8 infill boards for a solid fence and cut a pattern for the top if desired. Make your pattern cutting easier by clamping two or three boards together and cutting the pattern all at once. You may be able to buy precut boards at your home center.

3 Attach boards

Starting at an end post or a gatepost, fasten the infill to the rails with 2-inch coated screws. Fasten the top of the board first, plumb it with a carpenter's level, then fasten the bottom of the board.

4 Build the gate

Measure the opening for the gate and construct the gate using the techniques shown on pages 110–111. Mark the position of the hinges on the gate frame and fasten the hinges with coated screws.

5 Hang the gate

If the gate is small enough, hanging it may be a one-person job. Use blocks to support it (see pages 118–120). For larger gates enlist the aid of a helper. Fasten the top hinge first. Then line up the bottom hinge and mark its position on the post. Pull the hinge pin if the hinge style permits it and install the hinge plate. Fasten the middle hinge last. Mark the position of the latch hardware and install it.

BOARD-AND-BATTEN FENCE

A board-and-batten fence is a variation of the vertical board style but with the three-dimensional addition of battens on the surface.

The battens (generally 1×2s) help break up the expanse of the fence and add a small amount of texture that has a large impact on the way the fence looks. Board-and-batten construction is time-consuming and costs more than a plain fence, but the aesthetic return is high, making this fence and the effort to build it a worthwhile investment.

Build a board-and-batten fence

Build an edge-rail or flat-rail frame (see pages 50 and 52) with 6- to 8-foot bays. Mount the 1×6 or 1×8 infill, then fasten 1×2 battens on top of each joint.

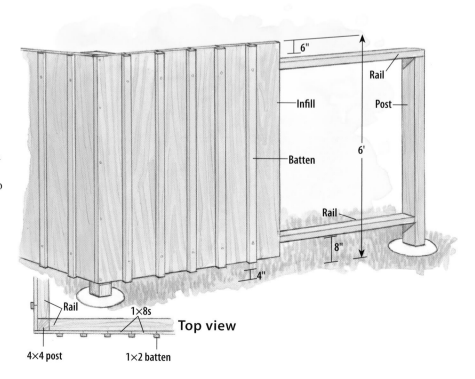

Top view

64

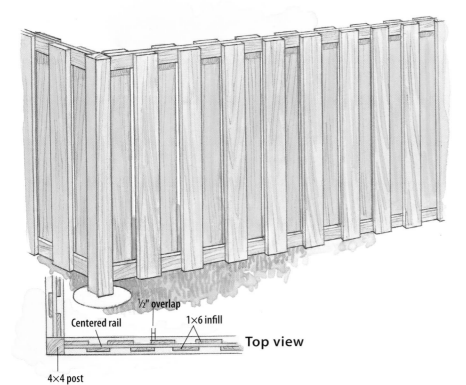

½" overlap

Centered rail

1×6 infill

Top view

4×4 post

Build a board-on-board fence

Depending on how much you overlap the boards, a board-on-board fence creates full or partial privacy. No matter what the spacing, this fence will protect you from the wind, breaking it up into little breezes.

In the style shown, the infill is fastened to each side of centered edge rails to create a fence that looks good from both sides.

Surface-mounted infill is easier to install but leaves more open space between the sides, decreasing the gracefulness inherent in this style. Inset infill is shown on page 56.

1 Construct the frame

Build an edge-rail frame with 6- to 8-foot bays, centering the rails on the posts (add a flat rail at the bottom if your design calls for it). Starting at an end post, fasten 1×6 infill to one side of the fence, using a hanging spacer to keep the boards at consistent intervals (page 58). Fasten the top of the infill first, plumb the board, then fasten the bottom.

2 Install infill on other side

Start the infill on the other side of the fence, overlapping the boards on the first side of the fence by ½ inch. Using the same techniques and the spacer, fasten the infill to the second side. The spacer will keep the boards overlapped consistently. Top off the fence with a top rail and a 2×6 cap rail if desired.

Horizontal rail fence

- **TIME:** Allow 2 or more days
- **SKILLS:** Site layout, digging, concrete work, measuring and marking, cutting, fastening
- **TOOLS:** Layout, digging, and concrete tools for layout and setting posts, carpentry tools for building fence

Horizontal rail fences come in a variety of styles, but all of them are relatively simple to build. Cut post tops to points or bevels to add style. Close rail spacing increases privacy and alternate rail widths add interest. Capped post-and-rail fences, an outgrowth of earlier styles, go well in contemporary settings and the cap rail strengthens the structure. Notched post-and-rail fences bring a classic ranch look that feels at home in many landscape styles. Rustic mortised fences (see page 74), usually with only two or three rails, are also adaptable to almost any landscape theme.

Material costs for a capped post-and-rail fence will run on the high side because of the large quantity of lumber required. Notched and mortised fences are less expensive but require more assembly time.

Always offset the rail joints on alternate courses. Prefinish the fence parts before assembling to make sure all surfaces are protected.

CAPPED POST-AND-RAIL FENCE

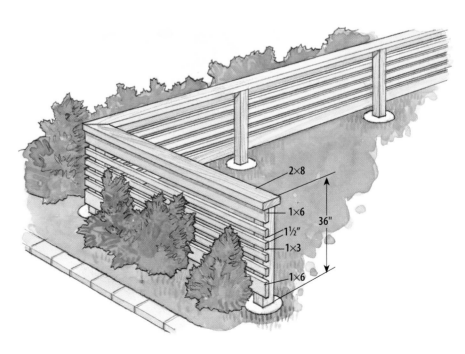

2×8

1×6

1½"

1×3

1×6

36"

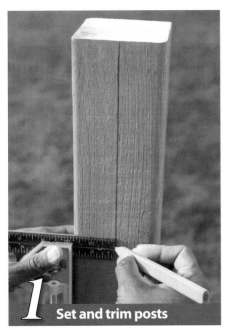

1 Set and trim posts

Lay out your fence line and set posts for 4- to 6-foot bays. Cut the posts level with each other. Using a combination square, mark the center of the posts. You can mark only the locations where the rails will fall or scribe the line down the length of the post. The line will ensure that you have joined rails centered.

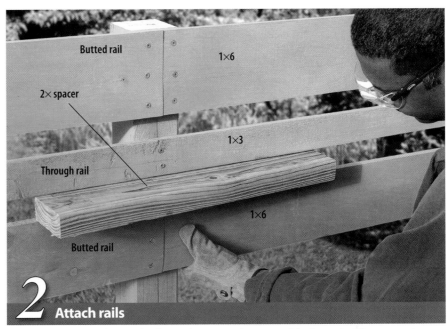

Butted rail

1×6

2× spacer

1×3

Through rail

1×6

Butted rail

2 Attach rails

Starting at the top, fasten the first rail flush with the top of the posts. Then alternate 1×6s and 1×3s, spacing them with a 2× spacer. Note that butted rails alternate with through rails every other board. Staggering the joints in this fashion increases the strength of the fence.

Drive angled screws to keep the mitered corner tight

3 Add the top rail

Measure and cut a 2×8 top rail, mitering the corners. Cut the miter first then cut the other end of the rail so that any joint will be centered on a post. Apply a thin bead of clear silicone caulk to the edges of the mitered corners, then fasten the rail to the posts. Pull the mitered edges together with angled screws. Wipe off any excess caulk with a damp rag.

HOW TO USE HORIZONTAL RAIL FENCES

- Defining spaces: excellent; they make attractive boundary markers
- Security: poor; low fences are easy to climb over
- Privacy: none; open rails permit open views
- Creating comfort zones: minimal; low height does not block wind; closely spaced rails can block drifting snow

Horizontal rail fence *(continued)*

NOTCHED POST-AND-RAIL FENCE

Notched post-and-rail fences take a little more time to install than other fences. In part this is because of the time it takes to cut the notches but also because you must level and set each bay individually. That way you are assured that the notches will be level with each other. The proportions of the fence will differ with its size and bay width. For a 3- or 4-foot fence, fasten 1×4 rails to 4×4 posts, 6 to 8 feet apart. For a taller fence, use 6×6 posts with 2×6s for rails. Buy 16-foot rails so you can span two 8-foot sections but be sure to offset the joints on alternate courses. Surface-mounted rails go up faster but are structurally weaker and less attractive even with staggered joints.

36" to 48"

Posts and rails
Post-and-rail fencing does not offer great privacy or security, but it is an attractive way to designate boundries. It fits architecturally with many building and landscape styles.

1 Form the notches

Cut your posts to a length that will allow you to set them deep enough for local code compliance and still leave 36 inches above ground. Clamp them together with pipe clamps, keeping the tops flush with each other. Mark the position of the notches on the end posts and snap chalklines across all the faces. Cut and chisel the notches (see page 40). Then cut the rails and prefinish them if desired.

68

4' level

2×4 temporary crosspiece

2×4 braces on each side keep top of post 36" off the ground.

2 Level first rail

Lay out your fence line, dig the holes, and set the posts in loosely (but not in concrete). Hold the first post plumb and fasten 2×4 braces at its base so the top of the post is 36 inches off the ground. Backfill the posthole with concrete, plumb the post, and let the concrete set up (it doesn't have to cure). Then hold

the second post upright and insert a 2×4 in the notches of both posts. Level the 2×4 and fasten 2×4 bottom braces to the second post. Backfill the second posthole and let the concrete set. Repeat the process for all posts and let the concrete cure.

Through rail

Butted rail

3 Attach rails

Distribute the rails along the fence line so they will be close at hand when you need them. Insert the rails in the notches, centering any joints on the post, and fasten the rails with coated

screws. Note that butted rails should alternate with through rails to add strength to the fence.

Basket-weave fence

- **TIME:** Allow 2 or more days
- **SKILLS:** Site layout, digging, concrete work, measuring and marking, cutting, fastening
- **TOOLS:** Layout, digging, and concrete tools for layout and setting posts; carpentry tools for building fence

Basket-weave fencing gives you an opportunity to create style with little effort. It creates interesting shadow lines, admits breezes, and maintains privacy but is not an inexpensive fence (especially with special-ordered infill). Choose the infill width carefully. Over a long fence line, wide infill boards (1×8s) can look overwhelming. Narrower boards (down to 1×4s) will add interest to the fence and make it seem less imposing. Because weave itself adds strength to the frame, you may not need a kickboard for rail support, but you can add one for appearance.

A 1×3 (or 1×2) spacer creates a center point around which the infill is woven. Benderboard, usually available in ½-inch×4 or ½-inch×6, often is used in basket-weave designs, but ⅜-inch-thick redwood is better. It stands up to the elements, imparts a warm feeling to the design, and is much easier to install than thicker stock. You'll spend more time building a basket-weave fence than a fence with surface-mounted infill but less time than on louvered or other fences with inset infill.

HOW TO USE BASKET-WEAVE FENCES

- Defining spaces: excellent; but can dominate small areas
- Security: poor; the weave makes the fence easy to climb
- Privacy: very good; even though the weave is open, you can't see directly through it
- Creating comfort zones: good; it softens winds and blocks sunlight

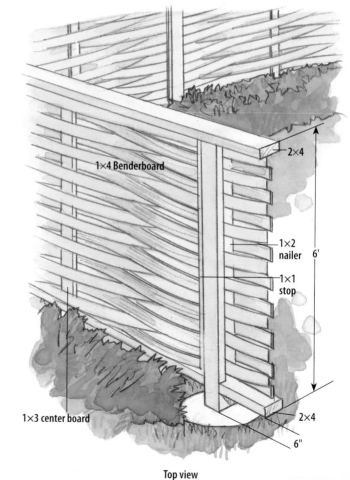

1×4 Benderboard

2×4

1×2 nailer

1×1 stop

6'

1×3 center board

2×4

6"

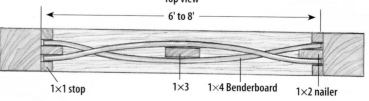

Top view

6' to 8'

1×1 stop   1×3   1×4 Benderboard   1×2 nailer

1 Build frame

Lay out the fence line and set posts for 6- to 8-foot (maximum) bays. Build a flat-rail frame (page 52), measure the space between the top and bottom rail, and fasten the 1×3 center board in each bay.

Position the board edgewise as shown here or flat as shown in the illustration on the opposite page, depending on how much separation you want between the woven fence boards.

2 Attach nailers to posts

At each post measure the space between the top and bottom rails (they might be slightly different in each bay) and cut 1×2 or 1×3 nailers to fit. Mark the center of all the posts and fasten the nailer to the posts with finishing nails.

3 Weave benderboards

With a helper holding one end of an infill slat snugly against the nailer on one post, wind the other end behind the nailer on the opposite post and mark its length. Cut all the infill slats for the bay to this length. Fasten the slat to the nailers at each end with 2-inch coated #8 screws or 6d or 8d box nails (angle them into the post faces). Then fasten the slat to the center board. Weave and fasten the next slat from the opposite side and continue hanging the infill until you fill the frame. Then finish the ends of the slats with 1×1 stops. Repeat the process for the remaining bays.

Louvered fence

- **TIME:** Allow 2 or more days
- **SKILLS:** Site layout, digging, concrete work, measuring and marking, cutting, fastening
- **TOOLS:** Layout, digging, and concrete tools for layout and setting posts; carpentry tools for building fence

A louvered fence imparts textural interest to any landscape. It can increase privacy without restricting summer breezes, filter the sunlight onto a garden bed planted in its shadow, and add security to a pool or patio.

Louvers splash light and shadow across the surface beyond the fence line. They produce partial privacy by limiting the outside view to only a portion of the yard at a time. But depending on the louver angle, the fence can become transparent to anyone moving at the right rate of speed past the fence (passengers in cars, for example, can often see through a louvered fence).

Louvers should be built with kiln-dried lumber to minimize warping. Add a kickboard so the weight of the louvers won't sag the flat rails. You can place 1×6 louvers on a 2×4 frame, as shown here, or rip louvers to fit. You can also use 1×4s on a 2×4 frame or 1×6s on a 2×6 frame, centering the louvers on the faces of the rails. The 1$^{15}/_{16}$-inch spacer shown fits three 1× louvers into every foot of bay length. You can fill any gaps at the ends with thin stock. Draw your pattern on ½-inch graph paper before you buy materials.

HOW TO USE LOUVERED FENCES

- Defining spaces: excellent; they make friendly fence boundary markers
- Security: very good; sturdy and hard to climb from either side
- Privacy: moderate; some visibility is possible from outside
- Creating comfort zones: good; louvers redirect winds and filter sunlight; featherboard does not make a good windscreen—the wind will vault it

LOUVERED FENCE

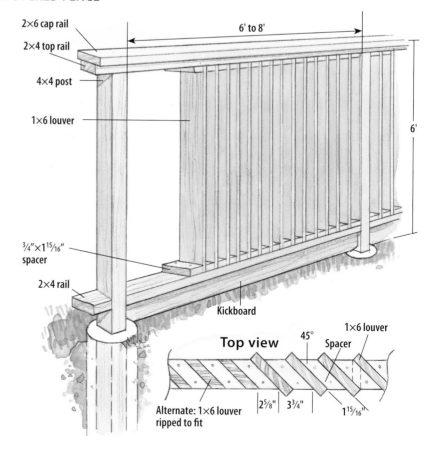

2×6 cap rail
2×4 top rail
4×4 post
1×6 louver
6' to 8'
6'
¾"×1$^{15}/_{16}$" spacer
2×4 rail
Kickboard

Top view
45°
1×6 louver
Spacer
2⅝"
3¾"
1$^{15}/_{16}$"
Alternate: 1×6 louver ripped to fit

1 Build frame

Lay out your fence line with 6- to 8-foot bays, dig the holes, and set the posts. Build a flat-rail frame (page 52) and cut the louvers to fit between the rails. If you're using 1×6 louvers, set them at 45 degrees with a combination square, centering it on the rail. If you're using 1×6 louvers, position the first louver with one corner against the post and the opposite lined up with the edge of the rail (see illustration, opposite). Toenail the louver to the bottom rail, plumb it, and attach it with screws driven through the top rail.

2 Add spacers

Cut and install spacers, fastening them to the top and bottom rail. As an alternative, you can tack a spacer to the rails, install the louver, and remove and reuse the spacer.

3 Install louvers

Continue installing alternate louvers and spacers until you fill the bay. Top off the fence with a 2×6 or 2×8 cap rail.

FEATHERBOARD FENCE

A featherboard fence is a closed louvered fence. The closed surface gives you maximum privacy with attractive shadows where the boards overlap. Build a flat-rail frame and fasten a set of 1×1 stops to the rails. Toenail the infill (1×4s or 1×6s) to the rails, and when the infill is mounted, fasten 1×1 stops on the other side.

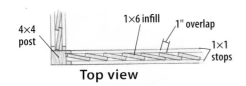

Top view

Mortised post-and-rail fence

- **TIME:** Allow 2 or more days
- **SKILLS:** Site layout, digging, concrete work, measuring and marking, cutting, fastening
- **TOOLS:** Layout, digging, and concrete tools for layout and setting posts; carpentry tools for building fence

Rustic rails with wedge-shape, tapered, or rounded tenons and premortised posts are available ready for installation. You also can cut your own traditional rails from raw logs. If you start from scratch, don't worry about minor mistakes; the rustic look allows you a certain amount of leeway.

Precut rails come in lengths of 6 to 10 feet and may be square (sawn rails) or wedge-shape (split). These fences tend to look better with shorter bays, but a 10-foot rail covers more distance with fewer posts (and fewer precut tenons) and is therefore less expensive. If cost is a factor, you may want to strike a balance on length.

The standard length for split, wedge-shape cedar, pine, or redwood rails with 4- or 6-inch faces is 6 to 11 feet. If you're cutting your own, you'll have a good deal of flexibility in how wide you make the bays.

Measure down from the top of the post to mark each mortise location so the mortises are in the same place on all posts. You should be able to locate the top rail 2 to 6 inches from the top of the post and the bottom rail 6 to 12 inches off the ground, with the middle rail centered between them. You must set mortised fences one section at a time—the rails will not fit in preset posts.

HOW TO USE MORTISED POST-AND-RAIL FENCES

- Defining spaces: excellent; they make attractive boundary markers
- Security: poor; low fences are easy to climb over
- Privacy: none; open rails permit open views
- Creating comfort zones: minimal; low height does not block wind; with closely spaced rails, they can block drifting snow

1 Cut and mortise posts

Lay out the fence line with 6-foot bays and dig the holes. Cut the posts to a length that will let you set them deep enough for code compliance and still leave 36 inches above ground. Cut a cardboard rectangle the size of the tenon and use it as a template to outline the mortise on the posts. Measure down from the top of the post the same distance so the mortises will all be on the same plane. Drill and chisel out the mortise.

2 Form rail tenons

Position the cardboard template on the end of the rails and outline the profile of the tenon with a carpenter's pencil. Mark the depth of the tenon on the side of the rails and use a reciprocating saw to rough-cut the tenons. You can narrow their ends and fine-tune them to fit when you install the rails.

3 Set posts and level rails

Set the first post in its hole and brace it 36 inches off the ground using the same techniques shown for a notched fence (pages 68–69). Test-fit the tenons in this post and the next one, shave them to fit, and set them aside. Backfill the first hole with concrete and let it set. Then set the rails in the next post, brace and plumb it with level rails, and backfill the hole with concrete.

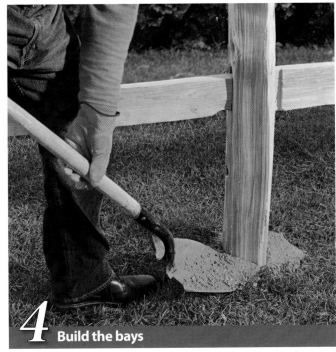

4 Build the bays

Continue setting each bay with the same techniques, leveling the rails and backfilling the holes with concrete.

RUSTIC MORTISE STYLES

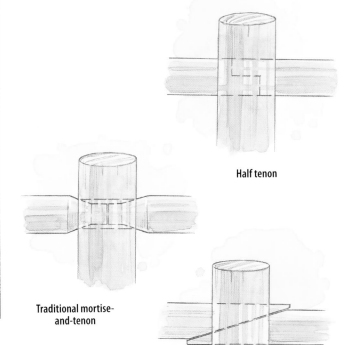

Half tenon

Traditional mortise-and-tenon

Overlap

Picket fence

■ **TIME:** Allow 2 or more days
■ **SKILLS:** Site layout, digging, concrete work, measuring and marking, cutting, fastening
■ **TOOLS:** Layout, digging, and concrete tools for layout and setting posts; carpentry tools for building fence

Picket fences are probably the most timeless and universal of all fence styles. They look equally stylish in a wide variety of landscapes, from Victorian to modern themes, augmenting the appeal of any landscape theme with their innate beauty.

HOW TO USE PICKET FENCES

■ Defining spaces: excellent; they clearly define any boundary with classic style
■ Security: moderate; they keep children and pets in or out, and pointed pickets can make it difficult to hop over
■ Privacy: none; open picket design permits open views
■ Creating comfort zones: minimal; low height does not block wind, but closely spaced pickets can block drifting snow

PICKET FENCE

1¼" 2×4

4×4

36"

2×4

8"

3"

1×4

Before you choose your picket style, visit your home center and look at preassembled 8-foot panels ready for installation. If you decide to save yourself some time with fence panels, make sure they are durable. Look for high-quality lumber (few knots and smooth finishes) and be wary of stapled frames. Millwork shops and some lumberyards will cut pickets for you for a fee, and of course you can cut your own designs too.

It doesn't matter whether you install the pickets on flush edge-rail or flat-rail frames, but if you like the looks of a flat-rail fence, you can add a kickboard to your design to minimize sagging. Most picket fences are installed on 4×4 posts and look best between 36 and 48 inches tall. Use 6×6 posts for fences taller than 5 feet (a taller fence starts to look like a stockade).

Before you put up a picket fence, experiment with picket widths and spacing to get the look you want. Traditional 1×3 or 1×4 pickets spaced 2½ to 3 inches apart will give you a classic look, but you can experiment to find spacing that pleases you. Draw fences to scale on ¼-inch graph paper.

First establish your bay width—6 to 8 feet is ideal. Then, to figure the picket spacing, decide how many pickets you want to spread across the bay. Multiply that number by the actual picket width and subtract the result from the bay width to find the total amount of open space. Divide this figure by a number one more than the number of pickets to find the distance between them.

Batten keeps pickets lined up.

1 Build the frame

Lay out the fence line with 6- to 8-foot bays, dig the holes, and set the posts with their tops 36 to 48 inches above the ground. Build flat-rail frames between the posts. Tack a batten 2 to 4 inches above the ground and use it to keep the bottom of the pickets on the same plane when you fasten them. Measure the distance between posts to compute the number of pickets you'll need to fill the bay. Recheck your measurements after installing the first few pickets and adjust the spacing if necessary.

2 Attach pickets

Distribute your pickets along the bay so they will be handy when you need them. Using the results of your computation for the number and spacing of the pickets, make a cleated spacer (page 58). Set each picket on the batten, space it with the spacer as shown, and fasten it to the rails.

77

Picket fence *(continued)*

Fashionable touches

Details can take a picket fence beyond the ordinary. Stepped points on the wide pickets and dentil molding below the post cap give this fence a distinctive architectural style.

Point of difference

Pickets often have square ends or straight-sided steeple points. Topping the pickets with slightly curved points and waists gives this fence a traditional look while adding individuality.

SCALLOPING YOUR PICKET FENCE

A scalloped fence usually looks better with pickets spaced closer than the traditional 2½ to 3 inches. Start experimenting on paper with your own design by spacing them about half a picket width apart.

Lay out the curve with a length of rope or decorator's cord about 2 feet longer than the span. Tack one end of the rope to the center of the picket or post at which the scallop will begin. Drape the other end over a nail at the opposite end of the scallop. Move the free end of the rope to adjust the curve and, when it's right (at least 1½ inches above the rail at the low point), tack the free end with another nail. Tape the rope in place and mark the curve on the face of the pickets with a carpenter's pencil. Mark the ends of the curve on the rope as you remove it so you can duplicate the scallop in the next bay. Cut the pickets with a jigsaw and sand the tops smooth.

Lattice fence

- **TIME:** Allow 2 or more days
- **SKILLS:** Site layout, digging, concrete work, measuring and marking, cutting, fastening
- **TOOLS:** Layout, digging, and concrete tools for layout and setting posts; carpentry tools for building fence

Latticework—thin, crisscrossed wood slats—has been used for screening for more than 2,000 years, and it's no wonder. It's lightweight and easy to work with, and the play of light and shadow over its surface is irresistible to the eye. Vines and climbing plants take to it readily, and its open surface lets in light and tempers the wind.

Prefabricated 4×8-foot wood or vinyl lattice panels with diagonal or rectangular grids are available at home centers and lumberyards. And with a little time and patience, you can make your own lattice. Wood lattice comes in several thicknesses. Lattice that's at least ¾ inch thick at the intersection of the boards is best for fences. The thicker pieces resist warping and cracking, reducing future maintenance— a good return on its slightly higher cost. Lattice goes up easiest and looks best inset in the frame. You can set it between stops, as shown, or into grooves cut vertically in the fence frame.

LATTICE FENCE

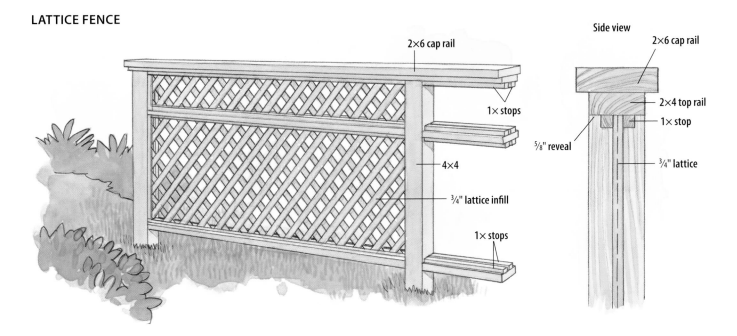

Lattice fence *(continued)*

HOW TO USE LATTICE FENCES

- Defining spaces: excellent; makes a neighbor-friendly, attractive boundary marker
- Security: minimal; lattice is easily broken
- Privacy: good; the fence pattern, not the view behind it, holds the eye
- Creating comfort zones: good; softens wind and filters sunlight

1 Build the frame

Lay out your fence line for 6- to 8-foot bays, dig the holes, and set and cut the posts. Install a flat-rail frame (page 52), adding rails to separate one panel from another. Mark the position of the rails on the posts (measuring from the top of the post down) and toenail the rails in place.

LOTS OF LATTICE

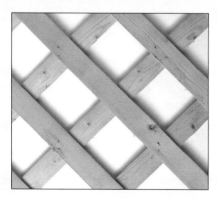

If you haven't looked closely, you may not have noticed that all latticework is not created equal. Lattice is manufactured from a variety of materials and textures; lattice openings vary in size depending on their intended use.

The toughest lattice is made with cedar 1×2s (¾ inch thick, 1½ inches wide). Technically this stock is neither lath nor strips. It lasts forever, will hold heavy vines without sagging, and should be used in large lattice screens, trellises, and arbors. Thinner lattice may prove to be an immediate disappointment in these structures.

Standard lattice thicknesses range from ½ to 1 inch at the intersection of the boards. Garden lattice usually has spaces 2⅝ inches wide. If you want a privacy screen, get lattice with privacy spacing—from ¾ to 1¾ inches wide.

2 Cut and fit stops

Add the thickness of the lattice and the inside and outside stops; then subtract the result from the width of the rails. Divide this result by 2. This is the amount of reveal—the distance from the edge of the rail to the edge of the stop. Mark the posts and rails at this width, cut additional rail stock to fit the frame, and fasten it to the posts with finishing nails. Cut and miter the outside stops, predrill them, and push the nails into the holes. This will make it easier to keep the stops lined up as you fasten them.

3 Install filler

To fasten any panel material, including lattice, tongue-and-groove stock, or plywood, cut the material to fit the opening of the frame and toenail it to the rails—not the stops. Set the bottom panel material in the frame first, then the top.

4 Fit lattice to frame

Cut the lattice panel for the top section to fit the frame and secure it to the rails and posts with finishing nails.

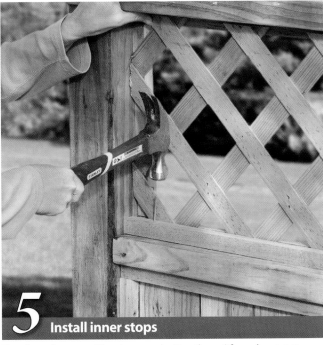

5 Install inner stops

Cut the other set of 1× stops and miter them (if you have not done so already). Fasten them snug against the lattice panel.

Siding fence

- **TIME:** Allow 2 or more days
- **SKILLS:** Site layout, digging, concrete work, measuring and marking, cutting, fastening
- **TOOLS:** Layout, digging, and concrete tools for layout and setting posts; carpentry tools for building fence

If you're looking for a way to integrate the architectural style of your house with other elements in the landscape, consider a siding fence. These fences allow you to duplicate exactly a number of different materials used on the surface of homes. Even if your house is finished with masonry or brick, a siding fence makes an architectural statement. Siding fences can provide total privacy if built tall enough, and those styles built with hollow cores, such as shingle and clapboard, help with noise control.

Hollow-core fences need a reinforced frame. Standard 2×4s or 2×6s will work, but you'll need studs to provide additional support as well as a nailing surface for some materials.

Siding fences cost more than other kinds of fencing. For example, tongue-and-groove lumber, like any other milled stock, is expensive. But if you're planning to paint your fence, you can save money by buying finger-jointed

tongue-and-groove stock. Finger-jointed millwork is made from shorter pieces joined with glued finger joints. It's strong but needs protection from the elements—finish it with high-quality primer and alkyd paint. Clapboard siding is more reasonably priced and construction will go quickly. Plywood, once fairly inexpensive, has risen in price, but building a plywood fence is an easy task.

For most styles start construction of a siding fence by setting your posts at least 3 feet in the ground (or to the depth required by local codes). Don't be concerned with aesthetics when spacing your posts; they are less visible in this design. Post spacing of 8 feet will work well with most materials.

Next build a flat-rail frame (see page 52) and, if required by the fence style, toenail 2×4 studs to the top and bottom rails every 16 inches. Use pressure-treated lumber throughout the frame—the cavity between the exterior and

interior faces will trap moisture so you need rot-resistant framing. When installing panel materials, use the methods for a plywood fence. Toenail lattice into the rails between 1× stops. For acrylic panel precaulk the rail along the stop with silicone. In most settings and with most materials, a cap rail enhances the appearance of the fence.

Plywood
A solid-panel plywood fence can look stylish despite the simplicity of its

Match the house
Siding fences are best for matching the architectural design of the home. The same siding used on the home can be used on the fence—one or both sides of the fence can be covered. These wood shingles provide complete privacy and the hollow core helps control noise.

1 Attach panels to frame

Lay out your fence line for 8-foot bays, dig the postholes, and set the posts. Mark the position of the first stops on the outer side of the rails and posts, using a reveal that will center the panel in the frame. Nail the stops to the outer side of the frame. Cut the panel stock to fit the interior dimensions of the frame and toenail it to the rails and posts. Build a flat-rail frame with a stud in the middle of each bay if you plan to build a fence with panels on both sides as illustrated on page 84.

2 Add inner stops

When you have fastened the panel to the frame, measure and cut the inner stops to fit, mitering the corners. Install the stops against the panel with finishing nails.

Use the same techniques to finish the remainder of the fence. Install a 1×6 cap rail, mitering the corner.

HOW TO USE SIDING FENCES

- Defining spaces: excellent; they make very attractive dividers, but will look imposing on a long fence line and will overwhelm a small space
- Security: excellent; but only if the fence is high, which may mar the overall appearance of the fence; impenetrable and difficult to climb
- Privacy: excellent; tall fences offer total privacy
- Creating comfort zones: moderate; blocks noise, sun, and snow; not a good windbreak—it's not tall enough and the wind will vault over a solid structure

construction. Because plywood comes in 4×8 sheets, fence designs with 4- or 8-foot bays will reduce or eliminate cutting the panels, and construction will go faster.

Only exterior-grade plywood will withstand the elements. Use ⅝- or ¾-inch sheets. They will provide the structural support required and will resist bowing in heavy winds.

Textured plywood siding is a good choice for fences too. It comes in several patterns. Simplify finishing tasks by using primed or prestained material.

Shingles

The highly textured surface of wood shingles gives a fence a rich and warm appearance. Shingles are sold by the bundle and vary in cost according to the grade. Relatively inexpensive No. 3 shingles have some knots and are specified for walls. No. 1 shingles are made for roofs and will cost much more. Cover the frame with ¾-inch plywood sheathing or nail 1×4 horizontal furring strips to the studs, spacing them at the length of the shingles (generally 15 to 18 inches). Fasten the shingles with 3d galvanized or aluminum box nails (two per shingle, ¾ inch from edges). Space the shingles ⅛ inch apart and stagger the overlaps 1½ inches. To keep the courses straight, snap a chalkline across each row at the point where the next course will begin.

Tongue and groove

Because its edges interlock, tongue-and-groove siding creates an extremely solid fence with a style that will suit almost any location. Shadow lines at the joints interrupt the surface with a subtle rhythm. The fence has an ordered, elegant overall appearance.

Clapboard and other siding

Nail a starter strip (as thick as the bottom edge of the siding) along the bottom of the frame. Then, working upwards, fasten the siding to the posts and studs with 8d galvanized nails. If you're not going to paint the fence, use aluminum siding nails.

For siding with a rabbeted bottom edge (Dolly Varden), beveled siding, or shiplap siding, install the infill without a starter strip. Attach these materials with 8d casing nails.

Posts match siding
Siding that matches the house has been applied to these gateposts. For more privacy and continuity, siding could be used on part of the fence.

SHINGLE FENCE

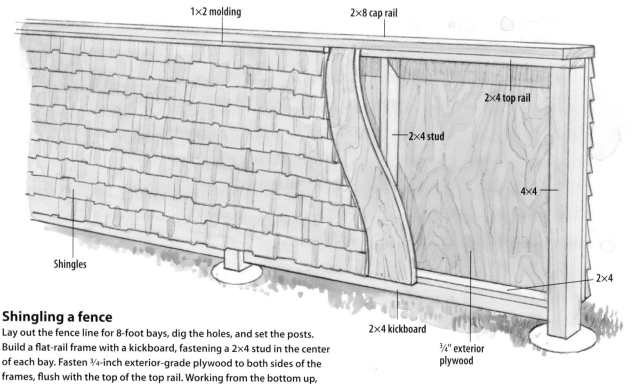

1×2 molding
2×8 cap rail
2×4 top rail
2×4 stud
4×4
Shingles
2×4
2×4 kickboard
¾" exterior plywood

Shingling a fence

Lay out the fence line for 8-foot bays, dig the holes, and set the posts. Build a flat-rail frame with a kickboard, fastening a 2×4 stud in the center of each bay. Fasten ¾-inch exterior-grade plywood to both sides of the frames, flush with the top of the top rail. Working from the bottom up, install cedar shingles. Finish the fence with a 2×8 cap rail and 1×2 molding.

TONGUE-AND-GROOVE SIDING

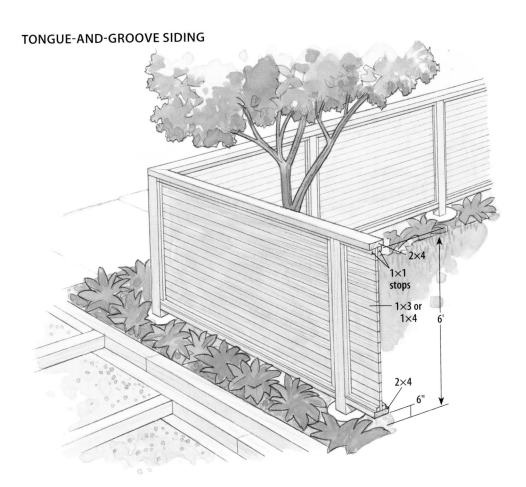

2×4

1×1 stops

1×3 or 1×4

6'

2×4

6"

Inset siding

Lay out the fence line for 8-foot bays, dig the holes, and set the posts. Build a flat-rail frame in each bay. Cut 1× stops and install them on the rails and posts. Then cut tongue-and-groove stock to fit the bay. Starting at the bottom, toenail the infill to the posts, tongue side up. Run a bead of polyurethane glue on the tongue of each board before fastening the next one. Continue until the bay is filled. Then install the stops on the other side.

CLAPBOARD SIDING

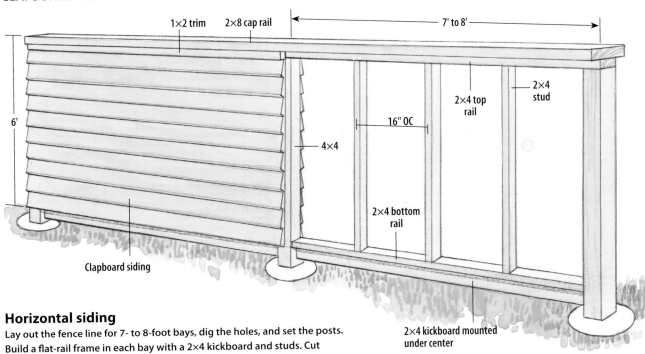

1×2 trim 2×8 cap rail 7' to 8'

6'

4×4

16" OC

2×4 top rail

2×4 stud

2×4 bottom rail

Clapboard siding

2×4 kickboard mounted under center

Horizontal siding

Lay out the fence line for 7- to 8-foot bays, dig the holes, and set the posts. Build a flat-rail frame in each bay with a 2×4 kickboard and studs. Cut clapboard siding to length and install it on one side of the fence. Work from the bottom up and offset the joints on the center of the studs and rails. Repeat for the other side and finish the fence with a 2×8 cap rail and 1×2 trim.

Prefabricated panel fence

- **TIME:** Allow 2 or more days
- **SKILLS:** Site layout, digging, concrete work, measuring and marking, cutting, fastening
- **TOOLS:** Layout, digging, and concrete tools for layout and setting posts; carpentry tools for building fence

Prefabricated fence panels make the job easier—all you have to do is lay out the fence line, set the posts, and hang the panels. The prefab sections eliminate many of the measuring and cutting chores. They're made for quick construction.

Once available in only one or two styles, you'll now find lattice, lattice on tongue-and-groove, offset board-on-board, dog-eared, and picket-shape infill. You should be able to find something to match your tastes as well as your time. Look for well-made panels—they might cost a little more, but they'll pay off in the long run. If your fence is sold as a kit it may include decorative post caps. Otherwise you can pick them up at your home center or chamfer the posts to help shed water.

1 Set the posts

Following the manufacturer's instructions, lay out and set the posts with the specified spacing. Let the concrete cure. Before installing each panel test-fit it between the posts. It should fit snugly. If it's slightly undersize that's OK, but if it isn't wide enough to hang in the brackets, add trim stock to the edges. Trim oversize panels on both sides with a circular saw.

2 Attach the brackets

Mark the position of the brackets on the posts as specified by the manufacturer and fasten the brackets to the posts. Take care when driving bracket nails with a hammer so you don't bend the bracket. Driving screws with a drill avoids that possibility.

Hanging prefab panels is a two-person job. Raise the panel above the top bracket and slide it down through the center bracket until it rests in the flange of the bottom bracket.

HOW TO USE PREFAB PANEL FENCES

- Defining spaces: good; neighbor-friendly models make attractive boundary markers
- Security: good if tall enough with solid or closely spaced infill
- Privacy: good; solid boards block views; board-on-board and lattice distract the eye
- Creating comfort zones: good; solid panels cast shadows and vault the wind; open structures filter breezes

4   Trim the posts

Install the gate with the hardware provided by the manufacturer or use the hardware of your choice, making sure your own hardware meets the same specifications as the hinges in the kit.

Mark the end posts for the height and snap a chalkline between them to mark the intermediate posts. Use a reciprocating saw to cut the posts.

Ornamental metal fence

- **TIME:** Allow 2 or more days
- **SKILLS:** Site layout, digging, concrete work, measuring and marking, cutting, fastening
- **TOOLS:** Layout, digging, and concrete tools, drill/driver, tape measure, level, screwdriver, hacksaw

With the exception of customized wrought-iron fencing available from specialty manufacturers, the metal-fencing market is now almost completely occupied by tubular steel and aluminum products. These fences are available in many styles (often mimicking classic wrought-iron designs) and prices. High-quality brands are virtually maintenance free.

Tubular metal fences offer an attractive alternative to forged iron. In the right setting they look sophisticated and ornate—from a distance some even look like ornamental iron.

Most installation packages include assembled infill sections (in 4- to 8-foot widths), posts, flanges, and the fittings to put them all together. Some systems are designed to accept rails in holes punched in the posts. Others are fixed with brackets mounted to the posts—a stronger method of mounting. Preassembled panels require bay-by-bay installation and setting of posts. Order the material and wait for delivery before you begin laying out your fence line.

If you need to shorten a section to fit a narrow area, cut the infill first. Then cut the rails to length, making sure you have the same amount of material on both ends of the panel.

If you're fencing a steep slope and want the fence to follow the slope, make sure the style you're purchasing can be racked (forced out of square) to follow the slope. If not you can install straight sections in a step-down design.

HOW TO USE ORNAMENTAL METAL FENCES

- **Defining spaces:** excellent; these fences set boundaries in style
- **Security:** very good if the fence is high enough and the infill spacing is narrow
- **Privacy:** poor; open infill provides very little privacy
- **Creating comfort zones:** poor; open infill does not filter wind or sunlight

1 Set the first post

Lay out the fence line, spacing the postholes as specified by the manufacturer. Set the first post in concrete, bracing it plumb and at the correct height with 2×4s, using duct tape to avoid marring the post's surface.

2 Attach the first panel

Slide the formed end of the rails into the brackets on the posts. You may have to jockey the panel so the holes line up all at once. Have a helper hold the panel in place so the rails don't pop out.

3 Install fasteners loosely

Using the fasteners provided by the manufacturer, secure the rails to the posts. If you use a cordless drill to drive the screws, set the clutch to the minimum torque setting. Do not tighten the screws completely at this time.

4 Place the next post

While one person continues to hold the panel in place, the other person should slide the second post toward the panel, fitting the rails into the bracketss in this post. Fasten the rails to this post loosely. Then set and brace the second post in concrete, plumbing it with a post level. Use duct tape to protect the braces as you did for the first post. Level the panel with a carpenter's level Tighten the rail screws with a screwdriver (not a cordless drill) and let the concrete set. Place the remaining posts in the same manner.

Ornamental metal fence *(continued)*

Installing metal sections on wood posts

1 Set the first post

Lay out your fence line, spacing the posts at the distance specified by the manufacturer. Dig all the holes, then set the first post in concrete, plumbing and bracing it (see pages 42–46).

Let the concrete set up (but it doesn't have to cure). Place the other posts in the holes but do not set them in concrete.

2 Install the first panel

Fasten the panel brackets to the first and second posts, spacing them as specified by the manufacturer (see inset). Then while holding the panel in place, slide the rails into the brackets on the

first post. Push the second post toward the panel so the rails slide into the brackets on this side also.

3 Install fasteners

Continue holding the panel in place and attach the screws loosely into the brackets. If you're using a cordless drill, set the clutch to the lowest setting to avoid overdriving the screws.

A point for security

Ornamental iron fencing can be elegant and provide substantial security. The finials on this fence add height and make the fence more difficult to climb.

Post level

4 Set the second post

Continuing to hold the panel in place, set and brace the second post in concrete. Level the panel with a carpenter's level; plumb the post with a post level. Tighten the rail screws with a screwdriver (not a cordless drill) and let the concrete set before mounting the next panel. Repeat this process until you have mounted the remaining panels.

Vinyl and synthetic fence

- **TIME:** Allow 2 or more days
- **SKILLS:** Site layout, digging, concrete work, measuring and marking, cutting, fastening
- **TOOLS:** Layout, digging, and concrete tools, tape measure, drill/driver, saw, level, screwdriver, awl

Fencing made from vinyl, composites, and other synthetic products installs relatively easily and is virtually maintenance free. It won't rot, rust, chip, or fade. All styles come as kits with precut parts. Most require some degree of on-site homeowner assembly, and although the basic steps for installation are generally the same (as illustrated here), each manufacturer has installation details to which you'll want to pay attention.

A few manufacturers furnish materials that require PVC cement or other adhesive for assembly. When gluing make sure the parts are clean and that you have plenty of ventilation.

As an alternative to a gravel base in postholes, you may be able to use sand. You can easily push the post base into sand, which allows water to drain away from the base. Some styles can be forced out of shape (racked) for installation on slopes.

HOW TO USE VINYL AND SYNTHETIC FENCES

- **Defining spaces: good;** use in a setting not requiring a great deal of structural strength and where low maintenance is desirable
- **Security: low;** characteristics vary with infill style, but most synthetic fences do not provide security

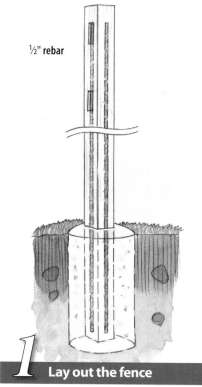

½" rebar

1 Lay out the fence

Lay out your fence line according to the manufacturer's specifications and dig all the postholes. Many vinyl fences call for end posts and gateposts strengthened with a concrete core. If your model requires it, insert ½-inch rebar down two opposite inside corners of the post and into the bottom of the hole. (You'll pour the concrete later.)

2 Set the first post

Set the first post, bracing it plumb and at the correct height as shown. Use duct tape or clamps to hold the braces on the post.

Backfill the hole with concrete and let the concrete set up (it doesn't need to cure).

3 Install the lower rail

When the concrete has set, insert the bottom rail in the holes in both the first and second post (but don't set the second post in concrete yet).

4 Assemble the panel

Assemble the panel in the manner specified by the manufacturer and install it in the bottom rail from post to post. Then push the top rail into the hole of the first post; slide it down on top of the infill and insert it into the hole in the second post.

ASSEMBLING VINYL PANELS

Assembly of the infill panels varies widely among fence styles and manufacturers. Some styles call for panel sections that slide together with grooved edges (above left). Others use panel sections whose edges are held together by a spline (above center). An assembly jig built from 2×4s (above right) makes assembly easier for many panels. Fasten the 2×4 blocks to the bottom rail so it just fits between them.

Vinyl and synthetic fence *(continued)*

5 **Set the second post**

While a helper holds the panel in place, set the second post in concrete, plumbing it and bracing it as you did the first post.

While the concrete sets up, install additional parts of infill or the cap rail as necessary.

6 **Complete panel assembly**

Complete assembly of the infill panel. This fence has an open top section made up of vertical members that fit into the rails. Other styles may not require additional assembly.

7 **Drive fasteners**

Most manufacturers require some kind of fastener driven from inside the post at an angle into the rail. Start with the clutch of a cordless drill at the lightest setting and finish tightening with a screwdriver. Using the same techniques, drive fasteners along the rail and into the infill as required by the fence instructions.

8 Fill posts with concrete

Mix a batch of concrete with a pourable consistency by adding a little more water than you would for a mortar mix. Then pour concrete into the end posts and gateposts to within 6 inches of the top.

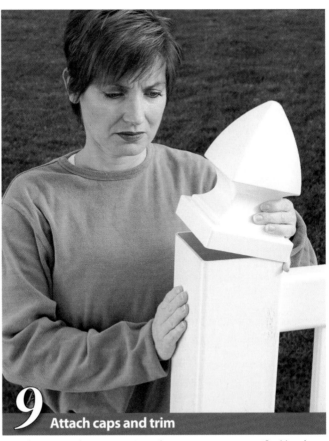

9 Attach caps and trim

Attach caps to the posts using glue or screws as specified by the manufacturer. If fasteners will be visible, use stainless-steel or other rustproof screws.

Racking a vinyl fence

Some vinyl and synthetic fence styles can be racked to a contour to follow a slope. Others are not intended for that purpose but can be modified. Rail-and-baluster styles are the most adaptable.

You might be able to miter the ends of the rails and lengthen the punched holes in the posts to change the angle of the frame.

The amount of adjustment you can make is likely to be small, however, and such modifications may void the manufacturer's warranty. If your fence is not rackable, consider a stepped fence layout along the slope (page 49).

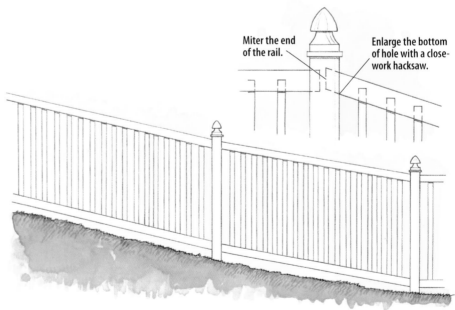

Miter the end of the rail.

Enlarge the bottom of hole with a close-work hacksaw.

- **TIME:** Allow 4 or more days
- **SKILLS:** Site layout, digging, concrete work, measuring and marking, cutting, fastening
- **TOOLS:** Layout, digging, and concrete tools, tape measure, fence stretcher, drill/ driver, level, pliers, screwdriver

Chain-link fence

You can hardly beat chain link for a long-lasting, almost maintenance-free fence. It is a great choice whether you need to keep kids or pets contained within a yard, to stop youngsters from wandering into a swimming pool, or just to define your property line in a no-frills, utilitarian way.

Constructing a chain-link fence is rather simple. You can fence in a moderately sized yard in a couple of weekends, and you'll find all the tools at your local fence supplier.

Most residential applications will call for a 4-, 5-, or 6-foot fence. These are standard heights for chain-link mesh (also called the fabric), but you can order heights of 10 feet or more. The mesh is woven from 6-gauge to 11-gauge galvanized steel (6-gauge is thicker and thus stronger), and you can also find vinyl-coated fencing in a variety of colors. Vinyl sleeves are available for the posts, so you can color-coordinate your entire installation. Black or dark green vinyl coatings blend well with most landscapes (and

may make the fence seem to disappear). Choose the mesh size to meet your needs—larger is cheaper, but smaller is harder to climb. Mesh 1¼ inches or smaller is recommended for swimming pool fences unless you insert wood or plastic slats into the fence.

Wood-slat inserts stained to resemble redwood make chain link an attractive backdrop for vines. Plastic and metal inserts also come in a wide selection of colors. One variety makes the mesh look like a closely cropped hedge.

TYPICAL CHAIN-LINK INSTALLATION

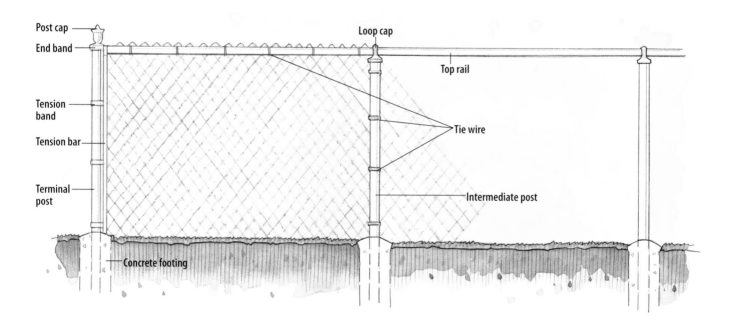

Post cap
End band
Tension band
Tension bar
Terminal post
Concrete footing
Loop cap
Top rail
Tie wire
Intermediate post

Plumb all posts with a level.

1 Set the posts

Lay out the fence, spacing postholes no more than 10 feet apart. Set the terminal (end) posts in concrete and let the concrete set. Then run a taut mason's line from the top of one terminal post to the other. Use this line to position, set, and plumb the intermediate posts at the correct height. Let the concrete cure for several days; there will be a lot of tension on the posts.

2 Assemble rails

When the concrete has cured, slide tension bands down the terminal posts and fasten one end band loosely at the top of each terminal post. Cap these posts with post caps and place loop caps on the intermediate posts. Slide the top rail through the loop caps and into the end bands, joining the rail as necessary with rail sleeves. Level the rail and tighten the end bands securely.

HOW TO USE CHAIN-LINK FENCE

- Defining spaces: good, but with a practical, not aesthetic, effect
- Security: excellent for small children; toddlers can learn to climb it, however
- Privacy: poor; open infill provides very little privacy; wood or vinyl inserts or plantings create privacy
- Creating comfort zones: poor; open mesh of chain link does not filter wind or sunlight

Chain-link fence (continued)

3 Unroll fence fabric

Tension bar

Unroll the chain-link mesh along the outside of the fence and lean it against the posts. Slide a tension bar through the end row of mesh.

4 Secure chain link at end

Tension bands

Tension bar

5 Stretch fence into place

Secure the bar inside the tension bands on one terminal post. Moving along the fence line, tie the mesh loosely to the top rail with tie wires.

Slide a stretching bar (or another tension bar) through the mesh about 3 or 4 feet from the next terminal post. Attach a fence stretcher or come-along (you can rent one) to the stretching bar and the terminal post. Tighten the mesh until you can

squeeze an opening no more than about $1/2$ inch. Unbend or cut the top and bottom links and unthread the surplus mesh. Slide a tension bar through the end and secure the tension bands to it. Tie the mesh to the top rail and posts.

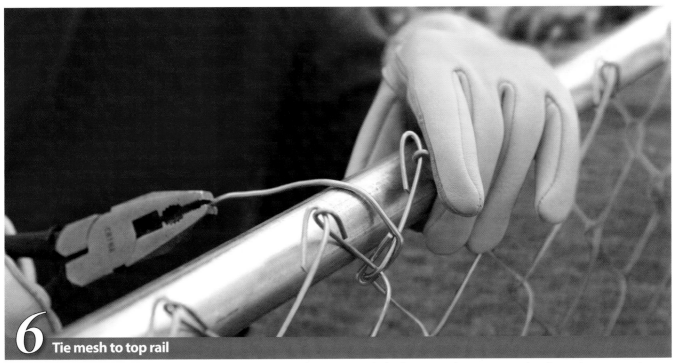

6 Tie mesh to top rail

Tighten any rail ties previously installed and secure the top of the fence with additional ties, one every foot. To install the gate, first attach the fittings to the gateposts, then hang the gate on the hinges. Finally, set the gate latch.

Dressing up chain link

You can improve the looks of your chain-link fence and increase the privacy it offers by inserting wood, metal, or plastic slats into the fabric. Cut the inserts to length and thread them through the mesh in a vertical or diagonal weave.

Virginia zigzag fence

- **TIME:** Allow 2 or more days
- **SKILLS:** Site layout, measuring and marking, cutting, drilling
- **TOOLS:** Layout tools, heavy-duty drill, spade bit and extender, hacksaw, sledge, chainsaw or reciprocating saw

HOW TO USE VIRGINIA ZIGZAG FENCES

- Defining spaces: excellent; they make stunning rustic boundary markers
- Security: poor; they can impede access but are easy to climb over
- Privacy: poor; open rails provide no privacy
- Creating comfort zones: poor; open rails and low height do not filter wind or sunlight

Virginia zigzag fences (or worm fences) were a product of rural ingenuity, traditionally built from logs split in a triangular shape. The combination of the shape of the rails and the angles of alternating courses kept the fence stable.

You can still buy 8- to 12-foot rails split from cedar or locust at some fencing outlets, but most rails today are sawn timbers. Sawn rails don't have the same rustic appeal as their hand-hewn counterparts. Rails are moderately priced, but a fence requires a lot of lumber—total material costs can be high for a fence that runs a long distance. Pressure-treated landscape timbers are a less-expensive substitute. Construction is fairly time-consuming.

1 Drill rail ends

Start by clamping (or holding) three 4×6 timbers with their edges and ends flush. Drill 9/16-inch holes in both ends. You'll need a bit extender to drill through this thickness.

2 Drive rebar into ground

Distribute the rails along the fence line and drive one 5-foot length of rebar about 2 feet into the ground. Thread one end of a rail down on the rebar and position the rail on the fence line. Drive a second piece of rebar through the hole at the other end of the rail and into the ground. Reset the rail on both lengths of rebar, supporting it with blocks or rocks. Then slide one end of a second rail over the end of the first one, position it at about a 30-degree angle (or the angle of your choice), and support it with a 4×6 block. Drive rebar through the hole and into the ground.

3 Stack rails for fence

Continue setting the lowest rails on rebar until you have finished the first course. Then slide the rest of the rails over the rebar to complete the fence. Drive the rebar flush with the tops of the rails. You could drill blind holes in the top rails to hide the rebar.

Kentucky rail fence

■ **TIME:** Allow 2 or more days
■ **SKILLS:** Site layout, digging, concrete work, measuring and marking, cutting, fastening
■ **TOOLS:** Layout, digging, and concrete tools, tape measure, chainsaw or reciprocating saw, lineman's pliers

HOW TO USE KENTUCKY RAIL FENCES

■ Defining spaces: excellent; they make stunning rustic boundary markers
■ Security: poor; they can impede access but are easy to climb over
■ Privacy: poor; open rails provide no privacy
■ Creating comfort zones: poor; open rails and low height do not filter wind or sunlight

Kentucky rail (also called double-post-and-rail) fences represent an early form of post-and-rail construction. You can angle a Kentucky rail fence across your property, but its double-post design suits it to straight runs. Originally the bays were built to a length that suited whatever material was on hand. Today's versions are more modular: 8- to 12-foot bays are typical. Use split cedar (a costly but attractive choice), treated round rails, or landscape timbers (4×6s are easy to handle). Set the posts so the rails will overlap by 12 to 18 inches. Rest the bottom rails on flat stones or fasten them to the posts. As an alternative to cinching the posts with wire, bridge them with wooden cleats screwed or nailed to the posts.

1 Set pairs of posts

Lay out 8- to 12-foot bays, locating the postholes so the distance between the posts will be about a foot shorter than the length of the rails. Dig the holes and set the posts plumb in concrete or tamped earth and gravel. You can keep the posts properly spaced by inserting a 6× piece of rail or a post between them. Remove the spacer when the posts are braced and use it for the next pair.

2 Place timbers

Cut 4×6 timbers to length (if not using precut stock) and distribute them along the fence line. Set the bottom timbers on alternate bays, supporting them with rock or brick to keep them off the ground. Then set alternate courses between the posts until the fence is complete.

3 Lash posts together

Wrap the top of each set of posts with #10 copper wire or soft iron wire and twist it tight with lineman's pliers. Cut the posts at 36 inches (or about 4 inches higher than the top of the highest rail).

SAWING BIG TIMBER

Cutting rustic split rails, sawn posts and timbers, or landscape timbers is a job for a reciprocating saw (page 21) or a chainsaw. The reciprocating saw is easier and safer to use and will generally make a cleaner cut, but the chainsaw is faster.

Exercise care when using a chainsaw. If you are not familiar with the tool, ask the dealer or rental agent to show you how to use it safely. Always wear eye and hearing protection; a hard hat with a face shield and hearing protection is best. Wear leather gloves, long sleeves, long pants, and leather boots when cutting with a chainsaw and stand balanced on the ground; never stand on uneven footing or a ladder.

Bamboo fence

- **TIME:** Allow 2 or more days
- **SKILLS:** Site layout, digging, concrete work, measuring and marking, cutting, fastening
- **TOOLS:** Layout, digging, and concrete tools, drill/driver, reciprocating saw, pliers

Bamboo is a fast-growing tropical grass that develops exceptional strength and weather resistance. These characteristics, along with the warm, soft golden color, make bamboo an excellent and unusual fencing material.

Bamboo fences are stronger than wooden fences and if properly installed will outlast many wood species.

Bamboo fencing comes in several forms: rolls in which bamboo stakes are held together with wire woven between them; panels in which bamboo stakes are stapled to horizontal rails; and panels woven with wire and attached to poles on both ends. Bamboo fencing is commonly 6 feet high and 6 or 8 feet long. Installation depends on how the fencing is constructed. You can even wire bamboo to a chain-link fence with galvanized wire threaded through the mesh about every 4 or 5 inches at top, bottom, and middle. Bamboo will deteriorate when in direct contact with the ground—keep the bottom 2 to 3 inches off the ground.

Some home centers and fencing supply outlets carry bamboo fencing or can order it from a distributor. Mail-order and Internet fencing outlets are other sources. Several manufacturers maintain websites, and you can order the fencing directly from them. All suppliers will provide you with design and construction details.

INSTALLING ROLLED BAMBOO

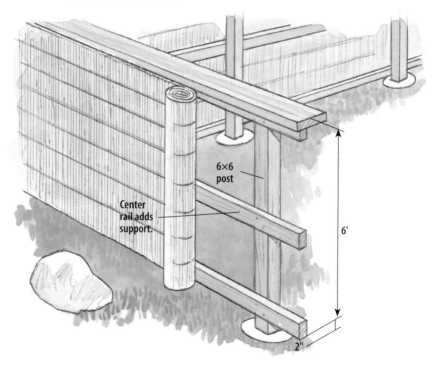

6×6 post

Center rail adds support.

6'

2"

Fencing with bamboo

Lay out the fence line for bays with interior dimensions equal to the width of the unrolled bamboo. Set the posts and build an edge-rail frame (page 50) with a center edge rail. Starting at one end of the fence, unroll the bamboo about a foot and tack it to the post. Unroll the panel to the other side and tack it. Then go back and fasten the panel to the rails, using the fastener recommended by the manufacturer and pulling the bamboo tight as you go.

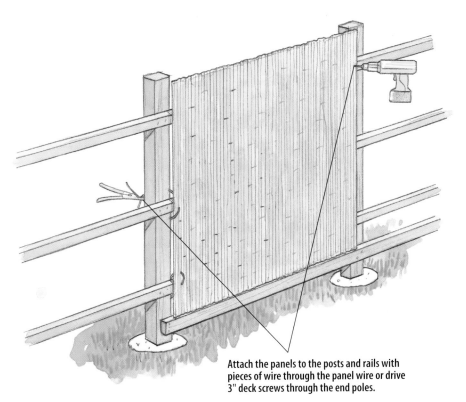

Wire or screw bamboo to frame

Lay out the fence line with the post spacing specified by the manufacturer. Dig the holes and set the posts. Attach rails to the posts. Tack a level batten along the bottom of the posts and set the panel in place. Wire the panel to the posts and rails as shown.

For panels with horizontal bamboo rails, predrill the ends of each rail and attach the rails to the posts with 2$1/2$-inch deck screws.

Attach the panels to the posts and rails with pieces of wire through the panel wire or drive 3" deck screws through the end poles.

HOW TO USE BAMBOO FENCES

- Defining spaces: good; bamboo gives a pleasant, informal feeling of enclosure
- Security: fair; bamboo is extremely strong, but lower-quality fences can be easily disassembled by cutting the wires
- Privacy: excellent; bamboo provides a surface closed to outside views
- Creating comfort zones: good; can soften winds, block snow, and provide shade

An exotic air

Bamboo fences and gates can add an Asian flair and privacy to a backyard landscape or water garden.

Variations on fence style

Fences allow an almost infinite variety in their design. Each member of a fence structure—the posts, rails, and infill—can assume different shapes that will conform to your sense of style and fit the design parameters of your landscape plans.

Posts are a prime target for design alternatives. Milled post caps or finials will spice up your design with little effort. Finials (available at your home center) come in a wonderful array of configurations made to fit 4×4 or 6×6 posts. Most come complete with lag screws that hold the finial to the top of the post in a predrilled hole. Other styles rely on glued dowels to keep them in place. To keep rainwater from rotting the top of the post, caulk the bottom edge with silicone before tightening the finial. Post caps (also readily available) cover the top of the posts completely and shed rain from the end grain. You'll find them fluted, corniced, and chamfered (some with metal covers)—in styles that match any fence design.

If you don't like what you see in the retail market, you can cut your own decorative shapes in the top of the posts. Chamfers are easily made by a tablesaw. So are any of a number of angled or beveled configurations and cornices. Rounded or globular shapes require a lathe. If you don't have the right equipment to decorate your own posts, you can probably find a local woodworker who will make them for a moderate fee.

Rail joints

How you join the rails to the posts can have a major impact on the appearance of your fence. Dadoes, through mortises, and channels (for panel or tongue-and-groove infill) will lend a touch of sophistication to your design. (They also will reduce maintenance costs because these joints are stronger than butt joints.)

POST CAPS AND FINIALS

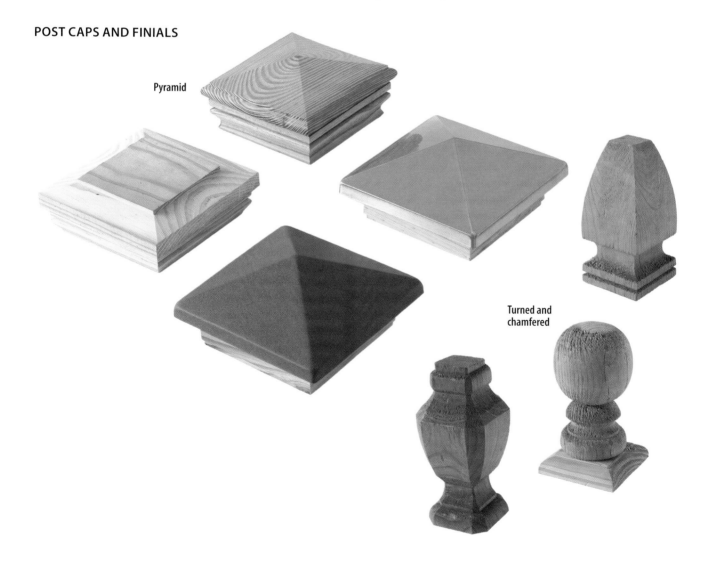

Pyramid

Turned and chamfered

RAIL JOINTS

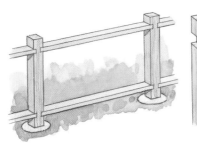

Channel joints
A dado cut along the length of rails and posts where panel fencing is inserted. Use it with or without trim.

Dado joints
Stronger than butt joints and make your fence look professionally finished. Use dadoes to mount edge or flat rails.

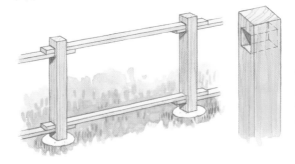

Through mortises
Must be cut precisely. Use them wherever you want to dress up a joint.

Infill design

Infill is the most prominent feature of a fence and unfortunately is often the last one considered for variation. Scalloping the infill is a technique not necessarily limited to picket fences. It also can increase the visual interest of flush-mounted vertical infill. So can letting the tops run wild. You can install the boards at completely random heights over the entire length of the fence or design a regularly repeating pattern.

Leaving gaps between the boards on a fence or alternating boards with slats and leaving open spaces between them is another option. This technique gives the infill a sense of refinement and a pleasing visual rhythm, an ever-changing play of light and shadow. Moreover it can make a long fence seem less imposing, and narrow spacing will help filter winds without compromising your privacy. It will also save you money because it takes less lumber than solid board designs.

Either of these techniques (or both) will help solve problems when fencing a small area. Alternating the infill heights emphasizes the vertical dimension of the fence. Varying the width of the boards and leaving gaps between them reduces the tendency of the fence to look massive.

No matter how you end up adding variations to your fence—especially to the infill—you should experiment with your design on paper before purchasing your material. Grab your ¼-inch graph paper and draw the fence to scale. Make quick sketches of various ideas on tracing paper and formalize your design to scale on the graph paper. There aren't any particular rules for this aspect of fence design. Style is often the result of creative choice.

WILD TOPS

SCALLOPED INFILL

Variations on fence style *(continued)*

Open tops

An unadorned board fence can appear massive and imposing, but you can soften that image by opening up the top of the fence. The look of a fence top will contribute as much to its overall style and appearance as the infill you select. Simplicity is the key throughout: Fence-top styles should provide a contrast, not a complication. Here are three ways to dress up your fence:

Blocked panel

In this variation 2×4 blocking at 3- to 4-foot intervals supports a 2×4 (or wider) cap rail. The blocks add an element of visual rhythm to the fence design and help keep the top rails from sagging.

Lattice

If you don't want a completely open top, install lattice. It affords some screening while it lets the light in and breaks up what otherwise might be an overwhelming stretch of tongue-and-groove or board infill. After fastening a 2×6 top rail spanning the posts, install lattice panels in a frame of 1× stops (see page 79).

Arbor

An arbor can bring an exciting contrast to any board fence. Make the supporting cleats from mitered 2×4s or 2×6s. The ends can be cut in decorative curves. Fasten the cleats to the post tops with carriage bolts. Predrill the 2×2 slats before attaching them to the cleats with screws.

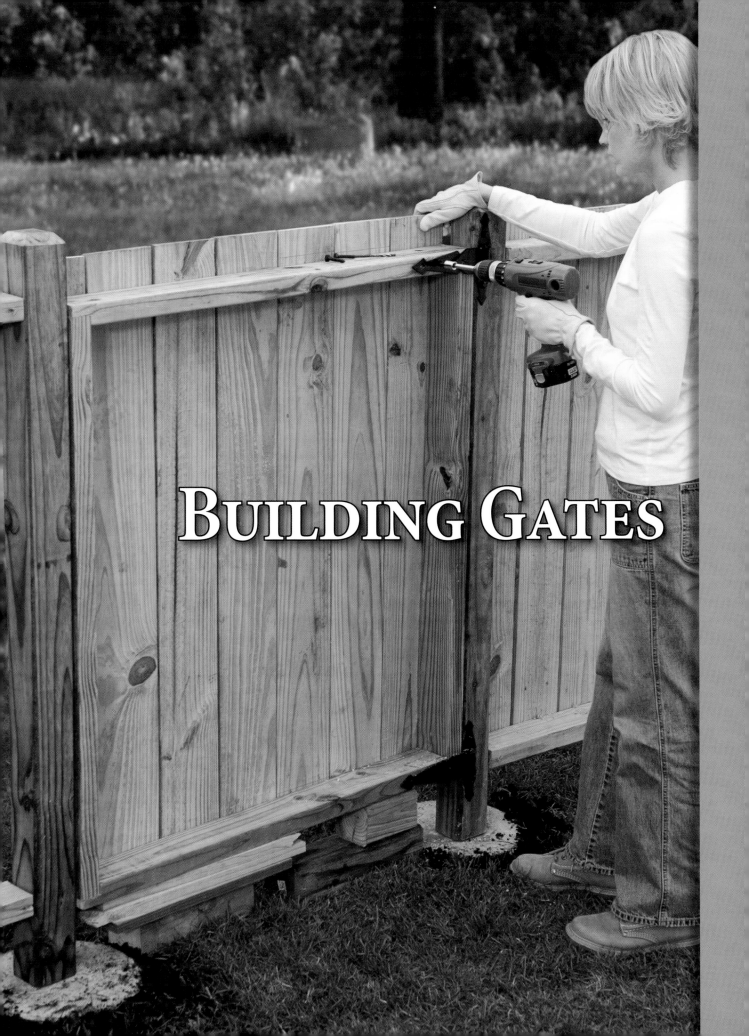

BUILDING GATES

Building a braced-frame gate

- **TIME:** About 2 hours
- **SKILLS:** Measuring and marking, cutting, drilling, fastening
- **TOOLS:** Tape measure, circular saw, jigsaw, handsaw, square, drill/driver, plane, chisel

Almost all gates need some form of diagonal bracing—which should be installed with the lower end of the diagonal on the hinge side. The gate shown at right employs double diagonals, although the second diagonal adds more to the aesthetics of the gate than to its strength.

A braced-frame gate can accept any kind of infill and therefore can be used with any style of fence. It's also rugged enough to support the weight of infill up to a size of 3 feet wide by 6 feet tall.

Measure the gate opening before you cut the framing. Take measurements between the posts at both the top and bottom. If the measurements are different, it means one or both of the posts are not plumb. Hanging a gate on tilted posts will make the gate look as though it's sagging (and, in fact, it will eventually sag). You can make a slight adjustment by shimming out the hinges to level the gate, but you should replace or straighten a post that's severely out of plumb (see pages 126 and 132). Once you have the measurements, subtract about ¾ inch to 1⅛ inches to give swing clearance (see page 118) for the frame and cut the framing to size.

Kiln-dried lumber is the best choice for the frame. Cut the rails the full width of the frame. Cut the stiles (vertical members) to a length that will put the gate rails on the same plane as the fence rails. You can use butt joints as shown at right, miter the corners for a cleaner look, or half-lap them for added strength. To make your gate even stronger, apply polyurethane glue to the joints before fastening them.

Lumber is rarely perfect so the prescribed number of infill boards may not fit flush with the sides of the gate no matter how carefully you measured and calculated. In every case it's best to cut the infill to length and dry-lay it on the frame. If it's a little too wide you can rip the boards or adjust the spacing.

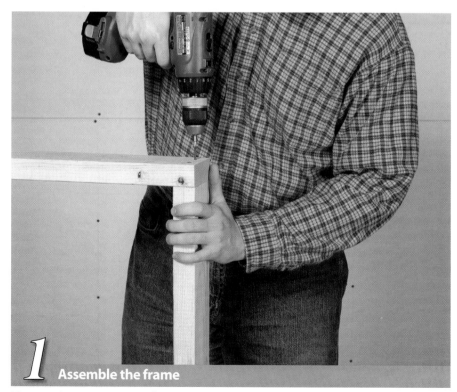

1 Assemble the frame

Measure the gate opening, allow swing clearance, and cut the frame sides and rails to size. Join with butted or mitered corners. Square the frame and fasten the corners with two screws in pilot holes. Screws into end grain are weak so reinforce the corners on a large gate.

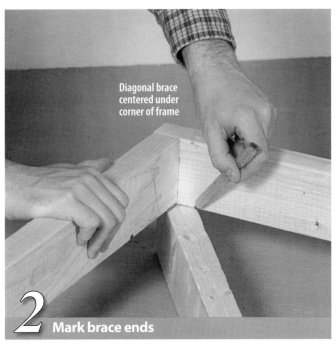

Diagonal brace centered under corner of frame

2 Mark brace ends

Support the frame on 2×4 blocks and center the 2×4 diagonal brace under opposite corners. Make sure the frame is still square, then mark the angles at the ends of the brace.

3 Cut and fit brace

Test-fit the diagonal brace in the corners. It should slide in snugly but without contorting the frame.

4 Cut second brace

Using the same techniques as you did in Steps 2–3, mark and cut the other diagonal. Cut a half lap in the center of one piece and use it to mark the other. Then cut a half lap in this diagonal too. The half-lap joint will allow the braces to fit flush in the frame.

5 Attach brace

Fasten the brace to the frame by driving screws through the corners into the ends of the brace. Then cinch the half-lap joint with a 2½-inch screw. Drill pilot holes for all screws.

6 Install infill

Cut the gate infill boards to the length required by your design. Fasten them to the frame and brace with 3-inch screws. Drill pilot holes for the screws.

111

Building a Z-frame gate

■ **TIME:** About 2 hours
■ **SKILLS:** Measuring and marking, cutting, drilling, fastening
■ **TOOLS:** Tape measure, circular saw, jigsaw, handsaw, square, drill/driver, T-bevel, pipe clamp

A Z-frame gate is a braced-frame gate without the sides. Because it uses a little less lumber, it's a little less expensive (and a little less strong) than a braced-frame gate. It is, however, a distinctive look reminiscent of the doors on farm structures.

Use kiln-dried lumber for the gate and lay out the infill to match the dimensions of the gate opening—less the clearances required on each side (page 118). If the width of the infill exceeds the final dimensions of the gate, you can rip the difference equally from the end boards. That way the infill will look balanced.

When you set the rails in place, position them so they're on the same plane as the fence rails. At this stage you can increase the strength of the gate by running a bead of construction adhesive across the infill at the center of the rail location. When the adhesive cures it won't give as much as the fasteners will under the stresses of the gate. Apply the adhesive to the diagonal brace too.

Spacers

Pipe clamp

1 Arrange infill boards

Measure the gate opening with the proper clearances, then cut and lay out the infill boards, spacing them to fit the dimensions of the opening. Square the boards with a framing square and clamp them together with a pipe clamp.

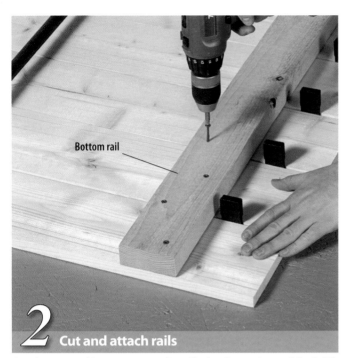

2 Cut and attach rails

Cut the top and bottom 2×4 rails to fit the dimensions of the infill (or slightly smaller if required by your design). Position the rails on the infill and tack them at each board. Remove the spacers.

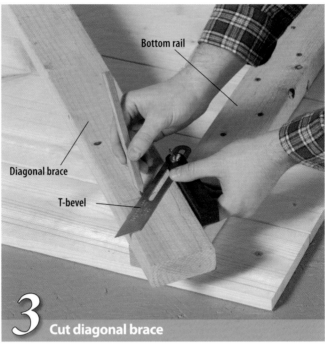

3 Cut diagonal brace

Keeping the gate square, set the diagonal brace on the infill (with the bottom of the brace on the hinge side and the top on the latch side). Mark the angles for the end cuts. Using a T-bevel will ensure that both angles are identical.

4 Attach brace

Tack the diagonal brace to the infill between the top and bottom rails. Then secure the joints by driving angled screws into the ends of the diagonal. Flip the gate over and secure the infill to the frame with two screws at each board.

Building a diagonal solid-core gate

- **TIME:** About 2 hours
- **SKILLS:** Measuring and marking, cutting, drilling, fastening
- **TOOLS:** Tape measure, circular saw, handsaw, square, drill/driver

A diagonal solid-core gate needs no external bracing. The diagonal orientation of the infill boards provides bracing against the stresses of the gate. The redwood gate shown at right also incorporates metal corner braces for additional strength.

You can build this gate with 1×4 or 1×6 boards (the scale of 1×4s will probably look more appealing) or tongue-and-groove boards. Tongue-and-groove stock will increase the strength of the gate—the friction between the mating surfaces will add to its stability. Make the gate even stronger by applying polyurethane glue to the tongues as you fasten the infill.

Because this design is inherently stronger than framed gates, it will span wider openings (which may require 6×6 posts), and the design is a good candidate for a double gate. Installing the gates with the diagonals running in opposite directions will increase the interest of the installation.

When you measure the gate opening, subtract the necessary clearances (page 118) and an additional 1½ inches to allow for the thickness of the trim. Be sure to install the gate with the diagonals running down toward the hinge side.

1 Assemble frame

Measure the gate opening and, allowing the proper clearances, cut the frame members to these dimensions. Lay out the frame on a flat surface and square the corners with a framing square.

2 Cover frame with infill

Keeping the corners square, cut corner braces and secure them to the frame on diagonal corners. Set the first piece of infill against the edge of one corner piece and mark the angle at which you will cut both ends. Cut the board at both ends and fasten it to the frame. Continue installing the infill until you have filled the frame.

3 Add face trim

Cut a two pieces of side trim equal to the height of the gate. Fasten them with predrilled screws driven through the infill and into the frame members. Cut top and bottom trim to the width of the gate minus the width of the top and bottom trim install them.

4 Add edge trim

Trim 1× stock to the thickness of the gate and cut the edge trim from it for all four sides to the dimensions of the gate. Fasten the edge trim to the frame with screws. Drill pilot holes for all screws.

Building a paneled gate

■ **TIME:** About 3 hours
■ **SKILLS:** Measuring and marking, cutting, drilling, fastening
■ **TOOLS:** Tape measure, circular saw, handsaw, drill/driver, square, hammer

A paneled gate is a framed gate that has the infill inside the frame instead of attached to the surface. It can incorporate one or more rails between the top and bottom rail, dividing the gate into sections.

Because this style puts the infill in the center of a frame, it adds visual interest to the gate. Even if the infill materials are the same as those in the fence bays, it will look different because it's not on the same plane as the fence. A lattice-and-board combination will lighten the visual appearance of the gate while preserving the feeling of security.

The frame must be strong. Some of the strength can come from the infill, if you install it solidly inside the frame with stops as shown in Steps 1–3. A gate as shown at right with floating infill requires strong joints and may need braces or reinforcements.

Install 1× stops to contain the solid infill. In effect the infill is sandwiched between the stops. Don't nail the infill to the stops, however; they will split. Toenail the infill to the frame.

You can use any material in any of the panels, but if you use lattice in the largest panel, you may want to add diagonal bracing. Vertical boards or tongue-and-groove infill will increase the strength of the gate because the surface of the infill works against the frame. Diagonal boards will provide the most strength.

To locate the stops subtract the total thickness of the infill and the stops from the width of the frame (3½ inches). Divide the result by 2 to determine the reveal—the distance from the edge of the frame to the stop. The reveal itself becomes an additional stylistic element because it adds another line and dimension to the design. You can butt-join the stops in the corners, but your gate will look better if you miter the stops. Arranging spacers around the frame as shown will make the installation of the stops more accurate. If you don't have spacer stock the same thickness as the reveal, you can rip some from scrap 1×4s.

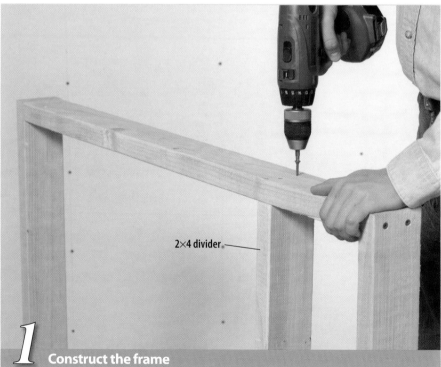

2×4 divider

1 Construct the frame

Measure the gate opening and cut 2×4 frame members to fit, allowing for the proper clearances. Fasten the outer frame members with butted, mitered, or half-lap corners. Square the frame with a framing square, then measure, cut, and install the 2×4 divider 10 to 12 inches below the top of the frame.

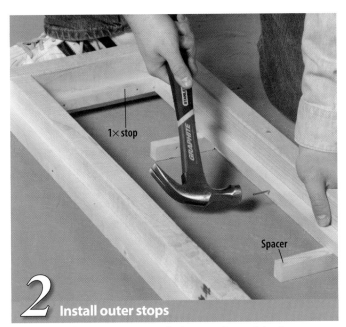

1× stop

Spacer

2 Install outer stops

Measure and miter 1× stops to fit the openings of the frame. Set spacers equal to the reveal around the frame. Setting the stops on the spacers, fasten all the stops with finishing nails. If you predrill the stops and insert all the finishing nails into them, nailing the stops will be easier.

3 Install infill

Cut the lattice panel to fit using a circular saw and lay it in the upper frame opening. Secure the panel with stops on this side.

Cut and install the lower panel infill, sandwiching it between stops as you did in the upper opening.

Hanging a gate

- **TIME:** About 1 hour
- **SKILLS:** Measuring and marking, drilling, fastening
- **TOOLS:** Tape measure, level, drill/driver, masonry bit or star drill for masonry installation, hammer, socket wrench

Hanging a gate proceeds in a fairly straightforward manner. To begin the process you'll have to jockey the gate into position. Start by supporting the gate within the opening. Set 2×4s under each end of the bottom rail (supporting an overhanging infill will only tip the gate one way or the other). Add 2×4s until you get the bottom rail within ¼ inch of level with the bottom rail of the fence. Then work tapered shims on top of both sides of the 2×4s (if possible) until the rail is in place. Next shim the sides of the gate.

Start with a thin, straight piece of 1× stock and insert tapered shims until both sides of the gate are set at the correct clearances (see Step 1 photo). Even though the gate may seem solidly wedged in the opening, have a helper hold it while you predrill the hardware holes and tighten the screws.

Most butt hinges will support the gate properly if you install them 4 to 6 inches from the top and bottom of the gate. T-hinges and strap hinges are made so their "straps" are mounted on the rails. Whatever kind of hinge you use, fasten it to the post first then the gate.

Swing the gate open and closed to make sure it moves smoothly, doesn't bind, and clears the opening evenly. If it doesn't, adjust the position of the hinge or insert shims under the plates. When you're satisfied that the gate swings properly, install the latch.

If you have designed your gate so that it stops on 2× stock (page 120) and you haven't fastened the stop, do so now.

Cut the stop 1 inch longer than the height of the gate and mark its position on the gatepost. Hold the stop on the line and predrill the first hole through the stop and the post about 1 inch from the top of the stop. Fasten the stop to the post with predrilled 3½-inch screws driven every 6 inches. On a wide surface, such as a masonry wall, use a 2×4 for the stop and mount it with countersunk lag screws.

½" to ⅝" clearance on the latch side

¼" to ½" clearance on the hinge side

1 **Position gate in opening**

Hanging a gate is easier with two persons, but you can do the job without a helper if you insert shims and blocks in the opening to support the gate. Using shims to keep the gate spaced properly is a good idea even if you have help. The shims ensure a proper fit. Measure, mark, and install the hinges, predrilling the holes for fasteners.

2 Attach latch to gate

Mark the location of the latch on the inside of the gate (the gate shown above opens out). Drill holes for the mounting screws and fasten the latch.

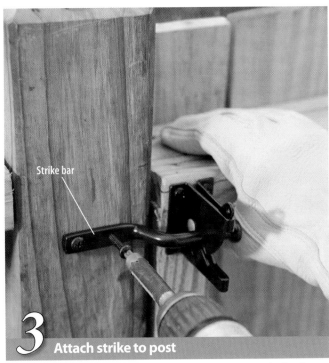

3 Attach strike to post

Hold the strike bar on the post and close the gate so the latch engages. Position the strike bar to allow free movement of the latch when opening and closing. Mark the mounting holes on the post, predrill them, and fasten the strike bar with screws.

Hanging a gate on masonry

1 Drill for anchors

Drill holes (counterbored if desired) in a 2×6 cleat and use these holes to drill locator holes on the masonry surface. Holding the cleat plumb, drill the locator holes with a hammer drill and masonry bit. Remove the cleat and drill holes in the masonry deep enough to accept the anchors. Insert the anchors in the holes and tap them flush with a hammer.

2 Attach cleat to post

Position the cleat with the holes lined up, insert a lag screw with washer into an anchors, and tighten the lag screw with a socket wrench. Install the remaining lag screws in the same manner.

Hanging a gate *(continued)*

STOPS FOR GATES

Infill on fence acts as stop

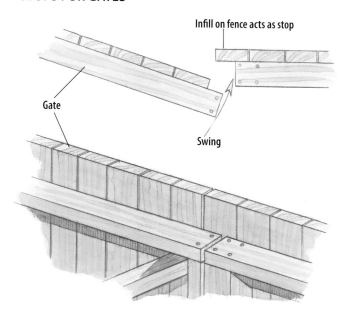

Gate

Swing

Gate infill is stop

In this style for a flat-rail gate frame, the gate closes toward the inside of the fence, and the edge of an infill board acts as a stop.

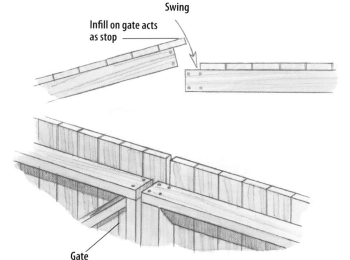

Swing

Infill on gate acts as stop

Gate

Fence infill is stop

In this style the gate swings to the outside of the fence, and when it closes, the extended edge of the fence infill acts as a stop. This method will work with both edge- and flat-rail gate frames.

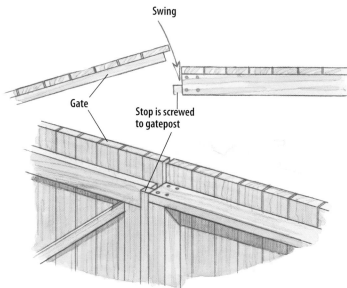

Swing

Gate

Stop is screwed to gatepost

Stop on back of post

If your gate swings to the inside of the fence, you can stop it with a board fastened to the inside face of the post if the fence and gate frame are both constructed with flat rails and surface-mounted infill.

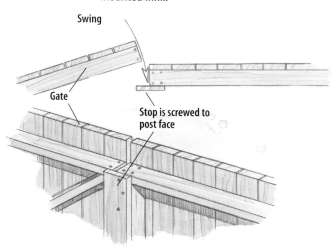

Swing

Gate

Stop is screwed to post face

Stop on face of post

This gate closes from the inside of the fence and is stopped by 2× stock screwed to the fence post. This method is limited to edge-rail gate frames.

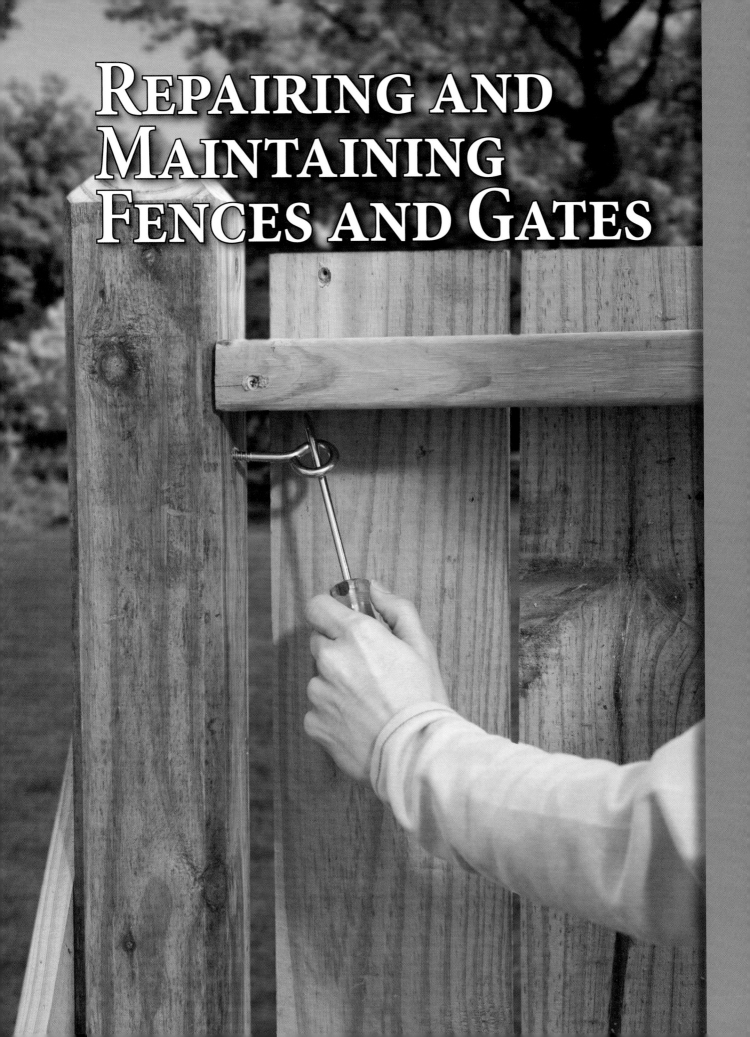

Repairing and Maintaining Fences and Gates

Repairing rails

■ **TIME:** About 30 minutes to repair 1 rail
■ **SKILLS:** Cutting, fastening
■ **TOOLS:** Hammer, nail set, cordless drill/ driver, tape measure, handsaw, circular saw, pry bar, clamps

Rails seldom deteriorate along the middle of a fence bay. Any damage they sustain usually occurs at an end. That's where rot begins—more often on the bottom rail than on the top because moisture collects on the fence and runs down and evaporates up from the soil. The bottom rail also tends to be more sheltered and is not able to dry out as quickly as the top rail.

One of the first signs of rail damage is loose fasteners. Before you rip off the rail, try resetting loose nails. At best this will probably turn out to be a temporary fix, because by the time you realize the fasteners are loose, the stress on the joint has probably enlarged the hole and removed enough wood fibers that the nail is left with nothing to grip.

If the rail works loose again after a couple of days, try removing the nails and refastening the rail with #10×4-inch coated screws (or screws that will be long enough to reach into fresh wood without going through the other side). As a last resort you can support the rail with several braces. These braces also are likely to be temporary—if a new

Set the nails

To tighten loose nails reset them with a nail set. If the rail is still loose, remove the nails and drive in longer nails or treated screws.

2×4 cleat

Metal T-bracket (install on both sides)

2×4 triangular braces

fastener won't hold the rail in place, it's a pretty good bet that the rail harbors some other form of structural problem and needs replacing. Bracing, however, will buy you some time, even though you may not consider it the most aesthetically appealing solution.

Removing and replacing a rail may take you an hour, but it won't take a great amount of energy. The most time-consuming aspect of this job is getting all the fasteners out. If the infill is fastened with nails, don't try to pry them out without first working from the backside of the fence to pry the infill away from the frame. Then go around to the front side of the fence and tap each infill board back on the rail. The board should move but the nail should not, leaving its head exposed. When you pry out the nails, slip a piece of 1× scrap under the hammerhead—it will increase your leverage and keep the wood from denting. Before you remove the rail, mark its location so you know where to put the new one.

Removing the rail does not require much finesse because it's damaged anyway. Don't try to pry it out—you may tear up the post. If it's screwed in place, remove the screws. If it's nailed give one end a couple of solid blows with your hammer (or small sledge), and it should fall away with the nails intact. Pull the rail from the other end with a twist. You can also cut through it near the middle and wrest the two ends free.

Replacing a rail

1 Remove the old rail

Remove fasteners on damaged rail only.

To replace a rail, first mark its location on the posts so you can install its replacement in the same place. Then remove the fasteners that attach the infill. To remove nails work from the backside of the fence and pry the infill away from the rail with a pry bar. Then from the front side of the fence, drive the infill back against the rail, exposing the nailheads. Remove the nails with a pry bar. To remove screws use a cordless drill. Once you have the infill fasteners out, remove the rail from the posts.

2 Position new rail

Repair fastener holes in the posts as necessary (see page 135). Then, to help you position the new rail, clamp a piece of 2×4 scrap on both posts at the location of the old rail.

3 Fasten rail in place

Measure the distance between posts (don't measure the old rail; it may have shrunk) and cut a new rail to this length. Set the rail on the 2×4 blocks and toenail it to the posts. Then go back to the front side of the fence and install new infill fasteners, keeping the infill plumb as you go.

Adding posts

■ **TIME:** About 3 hours to add 1 post
■ **SKILLS:** Measuring and marking, digging, cutting, fastening, mixing concrete
■ **TOOLS:** Digging tools, concrete tools, tape measure, circular saw, chisel, hammer, jack

A sagging fence bay may be an indication that gravity has gradually taken its toll, and the weight of the infill is more than the rails can support and remain level. This is a problem you might be able to remedy by jacking up the center of the bay with a hydraulic jack (just under the edge of the bottom rail) and installing a 2× kickboard. However, a sagging bay may also be an indication of serious post damage. If damaged posts are the problem and replacing the entire fence is not feasible, you can add a post in the center of the affected bay(s).

Mark the center of the bay and locate the new posthole. You can't center a clamshell digger on the hole because the fence is in the way, but you can come close, digging most of the hole with the digger and enlarging it from the other side with a round-nose shovel. Once you've dug the hole, you can set the post in it and mark the post for the location of the notches.

It's not critical at this step that the notches in the post are at exactly the precise height. What is critical is that their spacing is the same as the rail spacing and that the notches in the rails are plumb with each other, which will keep the post plumb when you set it.

What kind of notch you cut will depend on whether the rails are set flat or on edge (see illustrations below). You can notch the post with a circular saw, cutting kerfs and chiseling out the waste (page 40). The circular saw will also work when notching the rail, but the weight of the saw might make it difficult to work with when holding it upright. Using a jigsaw (and the same kerfing technique) will make this cut easier. Just make sure you cut the kerfs to the same depth.

When you set the notched post in the ground, tap it into the notches and tack it to the rails from the back of the post. You can level the rails with your method of choice. A hydraulic bottle jack is shown, but most screw jacks made for changing tires on cars will work also.

If you don't have a suitable jack, have a helper level the bay with a tamping bar levered on wood blocks. Keep the bay level with another set of blocks while you backfill the hole. Whatever device you use to level the bay, leave it in place until the concrete cures. When the concrete has set, strengthen the notches with additional fasteners.

1 Mark post position

To add a new post to a sagging bay, mark the center of the top rail and drop a plumb bob from the mark to locate the new posthole.

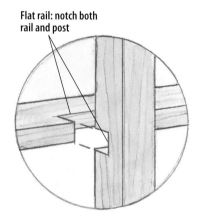

Flat rail: notch both rail and post

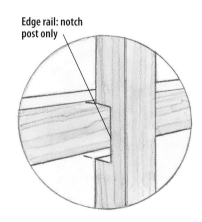

Edge rail: notch post only

2 Dig the posthole

Dig the new posthole and shovel in about 4 inches of gravel. Set the new post in the hole and hold it plumb against the rails. Mark the position of the notches on the post and cut both the post and rail notches. Set the post back in the hole and fasten the rails into the notches, keeping the post plumb. At this point the bay will still sag—you'll adjust it in the next step.

Cut new post to same height as existing posts.

Hydraulic bottle jack

3 Level rail and set post

Set a carpenter's level on the bottom rail and level the rail with a hydraulic jack. When the rail is level, shovel and tamp concrete in the posthole. Leave the jack in place until the concrete cures. Then use a line level to mark the new post at the height of the existing posts and cut the new post to the same height.

Replacing posts

■ **TIME:** 4 hours or more to replace 1 post
■ **SKILLS:** Digging, mixing concrete, cutting, fastening
■ **TOOLS:** Nail puller, digging tools, wrecking or tamping bar, chain, mason's line, post level, circular saw, drill/driver, hammer

If a post is rotted below ground and the aboveground section is sound, you can replace it with a new one or shore it up as shown on page 128.

Although shoring up a post is a repair that can last a long time, the repair will be obvious, and you may find its appearance distracting, such that replacing the post is the way to go. It essentially returns the fence to its original form. In any case, if the visible section of the post is damaged, you should replace it.

A post replacement requires stripping the infill from the bays on each side of the post and removing the rails. Because you'll want to reuse all this lumber, exercise some care when taking the bays apart. Slip a short length of scrap wood under your hammer, pry bar, or cat's paw when prying up nails. The scrap will give you a little more leverage and protect the

surface of the wood. Loosen the infill from the backside of the fence before pulling nails. If the fence is assembled with screws, make sure you remove all of them before taking a board down. Any screws that were overdriven when the fence was built may look like empty holes. When you try to remove a board that's still partly fastened, you'll rip the wood.

Pulling posts from the ground can be difficult work. You'll most likely have to dig to at least two-thirds of the depth of the post and usually to the bottom—at least on one side of it. No matter how much soil you remove, work the post back and forth before pulling it out. If the post breaks at the rotted section, you may have to dig it out in pieces, using a tamping bar to break it apart.

Scrap increases leverage

1 Remove fencing

To replace a post remove the infill from the bays on both sides of the post, then remove the rails. Add a piece of scrap under your pry bar to increase your leverage when pulling nails and to minimize damage to the rail.

Dig soil out around post base or concrete footing.

2 Dig out post

Dig out the soil around the post or around the concrete footing—as wide and deep as you can. The more soil you remove, the easier it will be to remove the post. Then work the post back and forth to loosen it from the soil. Pull the post free if possible. If you can't, pull it up as shown in the next step.

Tamping bar

Railroad tie or other
fulcrum

Utility chain
with hook

3 Pry out post

Loose posts will come free from the soil if you apply the proper leverage. Some can be pried out by driving a wrecking bar into the base of the post and pushing down on the bar supported by a block of wood on the ground. Stubborn posts may require the bar-and-chain device shown here. Fasten the chain tightly around the post and a tamping bar. Then insert a piece of railroad tie or other large fulcrum and push down on the bar to lift the post. If the post still won't come free, dig out more soil around it.

String taut mason's
lines to keep the new
post in line.

4 Set new post

To make sure your new post is lined up with the existing posts, tack mason's line to the faces of the old posts at both the top and bottom of the fence. Shovel 4 inches of gravel into the hole if necessary and set the new post in place. Brace the post plumb in both directions, making sure it just touches the mason's lines. Shovel in concrete and let it cure. Then tack a tight line to the tops of the existing posts and cut the new post to the same height. Replace the rails and infill.

Shoring up a damaged post

■ **TIME:** 3 to 4 hours for one post
■ **SKILLS:** Chiseling, digging, mixing concrete, measuring and marking, cutting, fastening
■ **TOOLS:** Digging tools, cold chisel, sledge, tape measure, reciprocating saw, drill, hydraulic jack, level

Shoring up a damaged post can provide a permanent repair if done correctly. For success most of the aboveground surface of the post must be damage-free. Before you start this job, support the post with temporary braces. That way you won't damage fasteners or the rest of the frame when you cut away the damaged section.

The most difficult part of this job is removing the concrete around the post. Not too long ago traditional post-setting methods called only for a concrete collar to keep water out.

Removing a collar will take a bit of time, but most will come away if you crack them with a cold chisel. You may even be able to crack the collar with a sharp blow from a small sledge. A hammer drill equipped with a cold chisel will also do the job. Wear eye protection when hammering or chiseling concrete.

If the post is set in a concrete footing, you won't be able to crack it. You will have to dig out the footing instead (see page 126).

At some point in this process, you'll have to cut the post—when you do it is a matter of preference and the requirements of the job at hand. Whenever you cut the post, use a reciprocating saw and cut it a couple of inches above ground (and above the rotted section).

Enlarging the hole sufficiently to remove the bottom of a post may leave a crater under your fence. If the hole is obviously larger than the concrete needed for the new post (and will leave a large concrete circle in your yard), drop in a cardboard form tube and backfill around the tube with soil. Then

1 Break up collar

Brace the damaged post to keep the fence from sagging when you cut away the rotted section. Break up any concrete collar with a small sledge and cold chisel, remove it, and dig out around the post. If the post is set in a concrete footing, don't try to break it up; dig around the footing. Cut the post above the rotted section and remove it and any footing. Enlarge the hole to accommodate the new post section.

Stub post angled to shed water

2 Set stub post

Cut a new stub post, then shovel about 4 inches of gravel into the hole and set the stub post in. Plumb it and brace it as necessary (you may not need the braces on this short a post) or clamp it to the old post if it's plumb. Then fill the hole with tamped concrete. Let the concrete cure. You can drill the holes in the new post before you set it in the hole or after the concrete sets up.

set the post in the form and tamp the concrete thoroughly when you pour it. You'll still need a layer of gravel under the post with the tube form.

Cut the new post from pressure-treated stock rated for ground contact. If you want the post to match, use the same species as the original post.

You can fasten the new post to the front of the old one, as shown here, or on the side of the old post. Attaching it to the side will allow you to clamp the two together, which makes plumbing the new post easier.

3 Attach stub to old post

If you haven't done so already, drill holes for carriage bolts in the replacement post (but not in the old post). Check the rails with a carpenter's level to make sure they are level. Raise them with a hydraulic jack to level them and leave the jack in place. Then use the holes in the replacement post as a guide to drill through the old post. Insert carriage bolts and tighten them, then remove the jack.

CHECKING FOR ROT

Moisture is the enemy of all wood and its presence in a wooden structure shows up as rot.

Rot will often—but not always—display itself as a deep black coloring in the wood. If your wood is black, it's sure to be beyond repair (and unsafe if present in a load-bearing or structural member).

To check for rot poke the surface with a slot-tip screwdriver. If the wood feels spongy and the screwdriver penetrates it without pressure, you'll need to replace the board.

Straightening a leaning fence

- **TIME:** About 1 hour per post
- **SKILLS:** Digging, mixing concrete
- **TOOLS:** Digging tools, tape measure, level, screwdriver, hammer, sledge, cordless drill/driver, come-along cable winch

Even a well-constructed fence can develop a lean over time. Strong winds and heavy rains can cause it to lean, as can poor soil conditions. And of course a fence with improperly set posts will eventually lean due to its own weight, no matter what. Bringing a leaning fence back to plumb is not difficult, but it does take time.

The key is digging on the backside of the leaning post sufficiently to provide space in the ground to move the post back to vertical. You'll need to dig down to at least two-thirds of the post depth to give it the freedom it needs. If you leave the excavation short, the bottom of the post will have to move against solid ground, and that risks snapping it. Concrete post footings increase the difficulty of removing the soil and straightening the post, but they don't make it impossible.

There are no specific guidelines or rules for determining how deep to dig. Onsite field experience is the best guide; you'll know when you try to move a post whether you have dug deep enough. If you get to a point where one or more posts are almost, but not quite, plumb, loosen the braces, dig

a little deeper, pull the fence back again, and rebrace it. With patience, and by working one step at a time, you'll be able to reset the fence exactly as it should be. When you're pulling the posts, you'll hear the fence creak, but if you hear sharp snapping noises, stop and dig some more.

A fence seldom leans in only one bay, so in most cases you'll have more than one post to straighten. Dig around all leaning posts—plus one more, even if the additional one is straight. Pulling the errant posts back into position may leave the next post overcorrected. Excavating this post will avoid this problem and allow the fasteners a little more give.

In most cases you'll have to work up and down the leaning section more than once. Trying to straighten the fence in one move puts too much strain on the wood, and you may end up with a broken rail. Drive metal pipes behind each post as shown in Step 3. That way you can move back and forth along the line without having to reset the pipe.

1 Dig out behind post

To straighten a fence section, start by enlarging the posthole opposite the side that is leaning down. Dig to the base of the post if possible, but at least two-thirds of the post depth. In most cases a leaning fence will be caused by more than one errant post—enlarge the holes of all posts that are not plumb. If the posts are set in concrete footings, enlarge the holes on all sides of the footings and dig to the bottom so you can move the footing along with the post.

Tighten screw eye to its shoulder.

2 Insert a screw eye

Predrill the side or back of each post for a ¼-inch screw eye. Insert the screw eye fully in the post and tighten it by hand as much as possible. Then lever it to its shoulder with a screwdriver inserted through the hole. If the leaning section of the fence is more than two bays long, fasten the screw eye to the innermost post first and start Step 3 at this post.

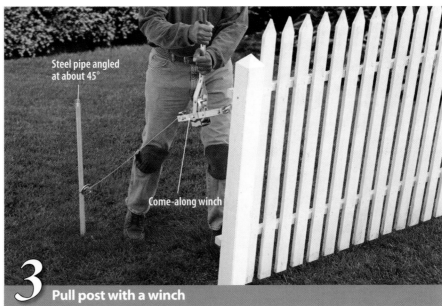

Steel pipe angled at about 45°

Come-along winch

3 Pull post with a winch

Drive a steel bar or pipe at least 2 feet into the soil about 4 feet back from the post and angled at 45 degrees. Attach one end of a come-along winch to the screw eye and the other to the steel pipe. Take up the slack in the come-along and reposition the cable on the pipe as high as possible. Tighten the come-along until the post is plumb and brace the post securely in this position. Remove the winch and plumb the remaining posts the same way.

Leave braces in place until concrete cures.

4 Reset post

Because straightening the remaining posts may throw the first posts out of line, check each post and replumb if necessary. Make sure all the holes are wide and deep enough to accommodate a sufficient amount of concrete, enlarging them if necessary.

Dampen the surface of any existing footings and backfill the holes with tamped concrete. Let the concrete cure and remove the braces. Retighten or replace any rail or infill fasteners that have worked loose.

Fixing sagging gateposts

■ **TIME:** About 3 hours
■ **SKILLS:** Digging, mixing concrete
■ **TOOLS:** Digging tools, tape measure, level, screwdriver, hammer, sledge, cordless drill/driver, sag bar, come-along cable winch

Gateposts are the hardest-working parts of a fence. The hinge post supports the weight of the gate and, in some situations, the added weight of young people swinging on it. If the hinges hold, all this abuse is transferred to the post. Both posts absorb the shock of the gate slamming shut thousands of times.

Gateposts sag into the gate opening or perpendicular to it, sometimes both, and not always just on the hinge side. If the post leans into the opening, you may be able to pull it back into place with a sag bar—a kit that includes a turnbuckle, a pair of threaded rods, and fasteners. In many cases pulling the post back with a sag bar will also pull it off plumb at right angles to the fence.

To straighten a post leaning perpendicular to the fence, you must dig around the post to give it space to move. This means digging down to at least two-thirds of the depth of the post. If the posts are set with concrete collars, break the collars up and remove them with a cold chisel and small sledge. If they're set in concrete footings, don't break up the footings—enlarge the hole by about one-third of its width and excavate to the bottom of the footing. If you find a rotted base when you dig, you'll have to replace the post (see page 126).

To keep the post from sagging in the future, shore it up with a concrete base. Excavating a trench between the posts and pouring concrete will create a solid base that helps anchor both posts.

1 Excavate around posts

To straighten leaning gateposts, dig around and between the posts so they will have space to move into when you straighten them. If the posts are set in concrete, dig around the footings.

¼" screw eye

Use turnbuckle to straighten post leaning into gate opening.

2 Plumb post

Push the post plumb or pull it into position with a steel pipe and winch (see page 131) and brace it. If the post leans into the gate opening, bring it plumb with a sag bar and turnbuckle. Brace the post in position.

3 Fill with gravel

Shovel a 4-inch layer of gravel into the excavation to allow water to drain out of it.

4 Pour concrete

Tamp the gravel base with a garden rake or tamper and then fill the excavation with concrete. Slope the concrete from the center to all four sides to let water run off. When the concrete cures, remove the braces but leave the turnbuckle if possible.

Repairing gates

■ **TIME:** 2 to 3 hours to square and rehang 1 gate

■ **SKILLS:** Measuring and marking, cutting, fastening

■ **TOOLS:** Tape measure, square, cordless drill/driver, screwdriver, pipe clamp, saw

A sagging gate can be caused by any number of failures in the gate system. Over time the gate may fall out of square, or its hinges can become loose or bent. The longer you let the problem go, the more damage the gate will incur. It is better to fix a minor problem as soon as you discover it than to have to rebuild and replace the gate entirely.

The most common gate problem is loose hinges, or more specifically, loose hinge fasteners. Before repairing the fasteners, however, take a close look at the hinge pins. Grab the gate by the top rail on the latch side and move it slowly up and down. Watch the hinge pins as you move the gate. If they move back and forth or if the fingers of the hinge rock against each other, the hinge is too worn for further use. Then look for bent hinges—a sure sign that the hinges are too small or are not positioned correctly on the gate or post. Gates that are more than 5 feet high or 3 feet wide need to be hung on three hinges—two won't do.

Replace all the hinges even if only one is worn or bent. One worn hinge means that the other has been working overtime and is soon likely to exhibit the same effects. When you install the new hinges, take a little extra time and mortise them into the posts and gate frame. Mortising transfers more stress to the entire frame and lightens the load placed on the hinges and fasteners.

When hinge screws have worked loose, it's usually too late to try to tighten them. By this time the screws have probably worn away too much wood, and they won't hold if you do tighten them.

You can move the hinges to a new position on the gate and post (and thus fasten them into fresh wood), but that can disrupt the balance of the gate as well as its aesthetic appeal. Instead remove the hinge pins and the gate and then remove the hinge fasteners from the gate and the post. Drill out the fastener holes as shown opposite and drive in glued dowels. The dowels provide a strong medium into which to drive the screw. If you replace the screws with longer ones, make sure the head seats properly in the recess of the hinge plate. A protruding screw head will come into contact with the other hinge plate and stress the gate when you try to open it.

If your gate is large and the hinges too small, you may want to increase the size of the hinges and use machine bolts to support them (see illustration below).

A racked (out-of-square) gate will show up with any number of symptoms. It may bind, the latch may work hard or not at all, and the vertical members of the gate frame may appear angled to the rails. All of these problems can be fixed by squaring the gate and reinforcing it so it stays that way.

The first step in reshaping the gate is to set a framing square on an outside corner and apply pressure with a clamp on the opposite diagonal. Tighten the clamp until you can't see any "daylight" between the gate frame and both edges of the framing square. Keep the corners square by tacking a 1× brace on an opposite corner. Then use one of the methods shown on page 136 to brace the frame permanently.

If the gate is square but binds when the weather is wet, plane wood off the latch side so it clears the post. Gates should typically have at least ½ inch of clearance between the frame and the latch post to allow for expansion.

If the latch binds in any kind of weather, change the placement of the latch or striker. And if the gate shrinks in dry weather to a point that the latch won't catch, relocate the latch or replace it with one that has a longer reach.

COUNTERBORING FOR BOLTS

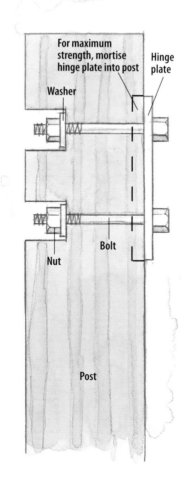

For maximum strength, mortise hinge plate into post

Hinge plate

Washer

Bolt

Nut

Post

Bolt holes

In some cases, especially with a heavy gate, it's a good idea to replace hinge screws with a hefty hinge and bolts. The heads and nuts of machine bolts can sit on top of the face of fence framing, but they will look dressier if you put them in counterbores. Use the techniques shown on pages 38–39 to drill the counterbore and the hole for the bolt. Make sure the counterbored recess is wide enough to accommodate a socket wrench and deep enough to accommodate the thickness of the nut and a washer (plus a lock washer if you use one). Tighten the nut until it's snug, then a half-turn more.

Repairing fastener holes

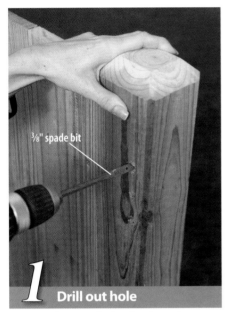

1 Drill out hole

To repair fastener holes that have become enlarged by loose screws or nails, remove the gate and old fasteners and drill out the holes with a ³/₈-inch spade bit. Because loose holes on the post likely mean loose holes on the gate frame, drill out the holes on the gate too. In both cases drill to a depth about one-half to two-thirds the thickness of the post or gate frame stock.

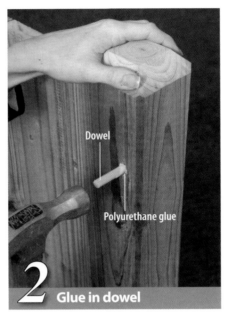

2 Glue in dowel

Cut ³/₈-inch dowels about ¼ inch longer than the depth of the holes and coat them with polyurethane glue (it's waterproof and very strong). Drive the dowels into the holes and let the glue dry. Saw the dowels flush with the surface of the wood.

3 Reattach hardware

Use a center punch or awl to dent the center of the dowel (the end of the dowel will be harder than the surrounding wood). Predrill it with a twist drill bit the same size as the shank of the new screw. Fasten the hinge with treated screws (nails may split the wood).

Squaring a gate

1 Pull gate square

Although there are several tools that will help you square a racked gate—a come-along winch, turnbuckle, or band clamp— a pipe clamp will give you the most control. Check the corners of the gate with a framing square to see which way you need to move the gate, then tighten the clamp.

2 Tack on temporary brace

Tack a piece of scrap across the corner of the gate to keep it square. Then remove the pipe clamp and brace the gate with one of the methods shown on the next page.

Repairing gates *(continued)*

Bracing options

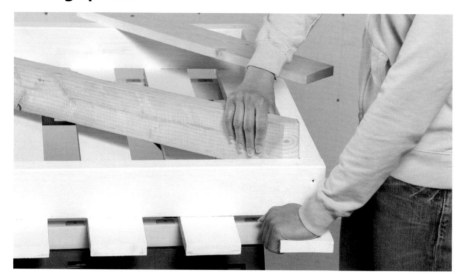

Diagonal wood brace

Measure the distance between the corners of the gate and cut a 2×4 with angled ends so it fits snugly in the corners. Fasten the 2×4 brace by driving angled screws into it from the outside of the frame. Remove the temporary brace and rehang the gate.

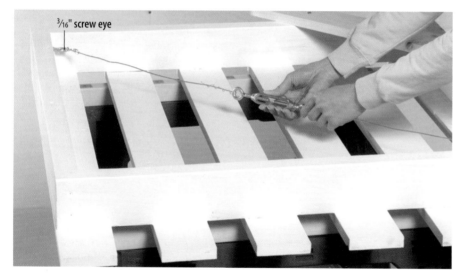

Cable brace

Screw 3/16-inch screw eyes into the corners of the gate and attach a turnbuckle between them. Tighten the turnbuckle until it begins to resist turning. Remove the temporary brace and rehang the gate. After a couple of weeks, check the corners of the gate with a framing square and tighten the turnbuckle as needed.

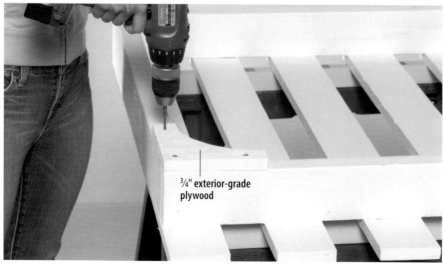

Corner brackets

Cut decorative corners from 3/4-inch exterior-grade plywood, then paint or finish them to match the gate. Fasten them to the corners of the gate with 1 3/4-inch treated screws. Remove the temporary brace, then rehang the gate.

Choosing finishes for outdoor projects

Outdoor projects must withstand a lot of abuse from the weather, which requires some planning and a durable finish.

Wood faces two formidable foes outdoors: moisture and the ultraviolet (UV) rays of sunlight. Different exterior finishes provide different degrees of protection against them.

Redwood, cedar, or pressure-treated lumber left unfinished will soon take on a weathered look, developing natural checks and slight surface imperfections. Depending on the species these woods will eventually turn some shade of gray. The color does not indicate deterioration, but weathered gray is a color some people do not find appealing. If you prefer the rich, natural hue of brand-new lumber, apply a product that protects the surface of the wood and helps it stand up to harsh outdoor conditions.

Here are your choices:

Clear finishes

Spar varnish, polyurethane varnish, water-repellent treatments, and penetrating oils shield wood from water while allowing all the color to show through. But clear finishes let UV rays penetrate into the grain. The wood cells react with these rays and begin to deteriorate under the film. The wood darkens, and the finish cracks, blisters, and peels.

A finish with a UV filter retards this reaction but doesn't prevent it. If you use a clear finish, select one that has UV absorbers (the label will tell you). Even with UV protection you'll have to reapply the finish at least every two years. If you wait until it peels, you'll face a tedious stripping job.

Stains

With light pigmentation, semitransparent stains let the wood's natural grain and texture show through. These stains are available in tones that closely match various woods. Brighter stains can either contrast with or complement your house, deck, or patio. Semitransparent stains come in both oil-base and water-base formulations that you'll have to recoat every year or two.

Semisolid stains have more pigment than semitransparent stains and offer more UV resistance as well. But they're not completely opaque. You can expect a semisolid stain to last about two years.

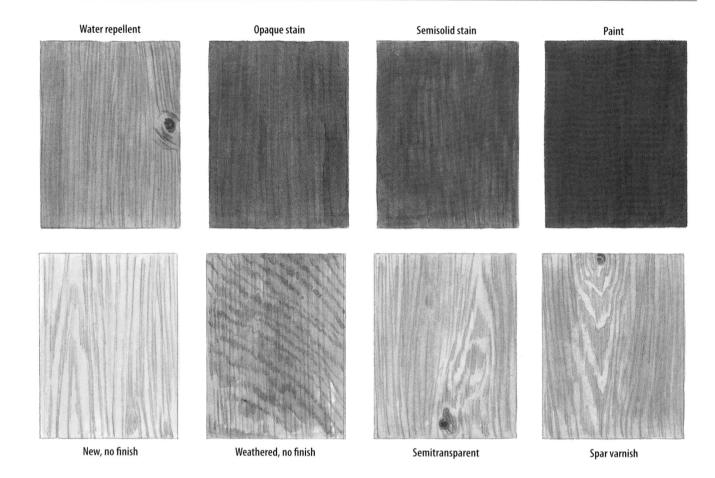

Water repellent	Opaque stain	Semisolid stain	Paint
New, no finish	Weathered, no finish	Semitransparent	Spar varnish

Opaque stains

Opaque stains, like paint, conceal the wood's natural color and grain pattern but allow some of the texture to show. They're available in a variety of natural-looking colors and brighter hues and with either an oil or latex base. You can choose either a flat opaque stain or a low-luster finish that's easier to wash.

Because the pigment in this type of stain is suspended in an oil or latex carrier, it's not designed to penetrate the pores of the wood. On horizontal surfaces especially, pigment that doesn't completely penetrate may collect, causing blotchy areas that wear off or blister. The California Redwood Association doesn't recommend using stains with a latex base on redwood products. Opaque stains usually need to be recoated every two years.

For treated lumber you may want to select a stain color compatible with the color imparted by the chemical treatment. Some chemicals will tinge the wood slightly, which can alter the effect of the stain.

Whatever stain or finish you use, experiment with different samples on scraps. Some manufacturers offer special 4-ounce samples that you can test before selecting a particular product.

Paint

Paint is rarely used on the top grades of redwood or cedar because it hides grain, texture, and color. But it can be your solution to hiding the hue of treated wood. Paint metal parts to protect them from the weather too.

Glossary

For words not listed here, or for more information about those that are, refer to the index (pages 141–143).

Actual dimension. The actual physical dimension of a board. See Nominal dimension.

Anchor. Metal device set in concrete for attaching posts to footings or piers.

Backfilling. Replacing excavated soil with soil, gravel, or concrete.

Batten. Narrow wood stock tacked to posts to help support level boards.

Batterboard. Layout tool made of a crosspiece attached to two stakes.

Bevel cut. An angled cut through the thickness of a piece of wood.

Bow. A bend along the length of a board that is visible by sighting along the face.

Box nail. Thinner nail than a common nail; drives easier and splits less.

Bubble plan. A plan that includes such nonstructural considerations as view, landscaping features, and traffic patterns.

Building codes. Community ordinances governing materials and construction methods.

Building permit. A license authorizing specified new construction.

Butt joint. The joint formed by two pieces of material fastened at 90 degrees.

Chamfer. To bevel the edges of a piece of lumber.

Check. A crack on the surface or edge of a board.

Clamshell digger. A tool with shovel-like blades and wooden handles used for digging postholes.

Cleat. A piece of lumber attached to strengthen a structure or provide an attachment point.

Concrete. A mixture of portland cement, fine aggregate (sand), coarse aggregate (gravel or crushed stone), and water.

Countersink. To drive the head of a nail or screw so that its top is flush with the surface of the surrounding wood.

Crook. A bend along the length of a board that is visible by sighting along one edge.

Crown. A slight edgewise bow in a board.

Cup. A curve across the width of a board.

Dimension lumber. Refers to boards at least 2 inches wide and 2 inches thick.

Dry rot. Fungal growth causing wood to become powdery.

Elevation drawing. A plan showing the vertical face of a structure, emphasizing footings, posts, rails, and infill.

Finial. An ornament attached to the top of a post or the peak of an arch.

Finish. Any coating applied to wood to protect it against weathering.

Flush. Level with the adjacent surface.

Frost heave. The upthrust of soil caused when moist soil freezes.

Frost line. The maximum depth to which the ground freezes during winter.

Grade. The surface of the ground.

Heartwood. The center and most durable part of a tree.

Kickboard. A board mounted under the bottom rail of a fence and perpendicular to it; used to strengthen the frame and keep animals from crawling under the fence.

Kiln-dried. Lumber dried to a low moisture content to reduce warping.

Lag screw. A screw with a hexagonal head that can be driven with a wrench.

Lattice. A material made of crisscrossed pieces of wood or vinyl.

Level. Perfectly horizontal.

Loads. Weights and forces that a structure is designed to withstand.

Mason's line. Twine used to lay out posts, patios, footings, and structures; preferred because it will not stretch and sag as regular string does.

Miter joint. The joint that is formed between two parts that have been cut at the same angle (usually 45 degrees).

Modular. A term describing a unit of material whose dimensions are proportional to one another.

Mortar. A mixture of one part sand, one part portland cement, and enough water to make a thick paste; used to set stone for patios, walls, and other projects and as grout between stones.

Nominal dimension. The stated size of a piece of lumber, such as a 2×4 or a 1×2.

On center (OC). The distance from the center of one framing member to the center of the next.

Plumb. Perfectly vertical.

Plumb bob. A weight attached to a cord used to show a true vertical.

Prefab. Short for prefabricated, meaning a structure completely assembled and ready for installation.

Pressure-treated wood. Lumber and sheet goods impregnated with chemicals for rot resistance.

Glossary *(continued)*

Rail. A horizontal framing member.

Rebar. Steel rod inserted in concrete for reinforcement.

Rip. To saw lumber or sheet goods parallel to the grain pattern.

Rise. The total vertical distance a slope or fence climbs.

Run. The total horizontal distance a fence or slope travels.

Sapwood. The lighter-color, more recent growth of any species of wood used as lumber.

Screening. Maximum opening allowed between railing members; distances vary by code.

Setback. The minimum allowed distance between a property line and any structure.

Shim. A thin strip or wedge of wood used to fill a gap between two materials.

Site plan. A map of your property showing where the fence will be located in your yard.

Small sledge. A sledgehammer, usually 2½ pounds, used where more weight than a carpenter's hammer is needed.

Square. A corner that forms a perfect 90-degree angle.

Stop. 1× or 2× lumber attached to rails to form a frame for inset infill. Also the board that stops the swing of a gate.

Strike. The part of a gate latch fastened to the post.

3–4–5 triangle. An easy, mathematical way to check square on a large scale.

Toenail. To drive a screw or nail at an angle.

Try square. A tool with a blade and handle fixed at a right angle used to determine square.

Water level. Two clear plastic tubes attached to a hose used for establishing level over long distances.

Zoning requirements. Ordinances that regulate the use of property and structure sizes.

METRIC CONVERSIONS

U.S. Units to Metric Equivalents			Metric Units to U.S. Equivalents		
To convert from	**Multiply by**	**To get**	**To convert from**	**Multiply by**	**To get**
Inches	25.4	Millimeters	Millimeters	0.0394	Inches
Inches	2.54	Centimeters	Centimeters	0.3937	Inches
Feet	30.48	Centimeters	Centimeters	0.0328	Feet
Feet	0.3048	Meters	Meters	3.2808	Feet
Yards	0.9144	Meters	Meters	1.0936	Yards
Square inches	6.4516	Square centimeters	Square centimeters	0.1550	Square inches
Square feet	0.0929	Square meters	Square meters	10.764	Square feet
Square yards	0.8361	Square meters	Square meters	1.1960	Square yards
Acres	0.4047	Hectares	Hectares	2.4711	Acres
Cubic inches	16.387	Cubic centimeters	Cubic centimeters	0.0610	Cubic inches
Cubic feet	0.0283	Cubic meters	Cubic meters	35.315	Cubic feet
Cubic feet	28.316	Liters	Liters	0.0353	Cubic feet
Cubic yards	0.7646	Cubic meters	Cubic meters	1.308	Cubic yards
Cubic yards	764.55	Liters	Liters	0.0013	Cubic yards

To convert from degrees Fahrenheit (F) to degrees Celsius (C), first subtract 32, then multiply by 5/9.

To convert from degrees Celsius to degrees Fahrenheit, multiply by 9/5, then add 32.

Index

A

Angles, marking, 33
Arbor, 108
Auger, 22–23

B

Backyard fences, 6–7
Bamboo fence, 104–105
Basket-weave fence, 70–71
Benderboard, 70–71
Bevels, cutting, 35
Blocked panel fence top, 108
Board-and-batten fence, 64
Board foot, 24
Board-on-board fence, 57, 65
Bolts, 30, 39, 134
Boundary line fences, 15
Braced-frame gate, 110–111
Bracing
    cable, 136
    corner, 136
    diagonal wood, 136
    for leaning fence, 131
    rails, 122
Brackets, 30
Building codes, 7
Building fences, 61–108
Building gates, 109–120
Building techniques, 31–60

C

Cable brace, 136
Cap rail, 52–53
Capped post-and-rail fence, 66–67
Caps, post, 106
Carriage bolt, 39
Caulk, 45
Cedar, 25
Chain-link fence, 8–9, 27, 96–99
Channel joint, 107
Circular saw, 19, 34–35, 55
Clamps, 18, 21, 97, 112, 123, 135
Clapboard siding, 84–85
Combination square, 19, 40–41
Concrete, 45, 95, 97
Contour fencing, 48–49
Corner brackets, 136
Corners, squaring, 42
Counterboring, 38, 134

Covenants and deed restrictions, 7
Crosscuts
    with circular saw, 34
    marking, 32
Curved fences, 47, 59
Cypress, 25

D

Dado joints, 107
Deer, excluding, 9
Diagonal solid-core gate, 114–115
Dog fence, 8
Double post-and-rail fence, 102–103
Drills and drilling, 19, 20, 36, 38

E

Edge-rail fence frame, 50–51
Electronic fencing, 8

F

Face-nailing, 37
Fastener holes, repairing, 135
Fasteners
    fence, 30
    for latches and hinges, 29
Fastening, 36–39
Featherboard fence, 73
Fence boards, 62
Fence-top styles, 108
Fence types
    bamboo, 104–105
    basket-weave, 70–71
    board-and-batten, 64
    board-on-board, 57, 65
    capped post-and-rail, 66–67
    chain-link, 8–9, 27, 96–99
    featherboard, 73
    horizontal rail, 66–69
    Kentucky rail, 102–103
    lattice, 10–11, 79–81
    louvered, 11, 72–73
    mortised post-and-rail, 74–75
    notched post-and-rail, 68–69
    ornamental metal, 88–91
    picket, 76–78
    prefabricated panel, 86–87
    privacy, 10–11
    security, 8–9
    siding, 82–85
    solid, 9, 12, 62–64
    vertical board, 62–65

vinyl and synthetic, 27, 92–95
Virginia zigzag, 100–101
Finishes
    clear, 137
    paint, 138
    stains, 137–138
Flat-rail frame, 52–53
Frame
    edge-rail, 50–51
    flat-rail, 52–53
Framing square, 19, 33
Front yard fences, 6

G

Gateposts, 14–15, 132–133
Gates
    braced-frame, 110–111
    bracing, 111, 113, 136
    building, 109–120
    designing, 14–16
    diagonal solid-core, 114–115
    hanging, 64, 118–120
    hardware, 15, 28–29, 118–119
    opening, 15
    paneled, 116–117
    repairs, 134–136
    sagging posts, 132–133
    squaring, 134, 135
    stops, 120
    structural system, 14
    swing, 15
    tips for construction, 117
    for vertical board fence, 64
    Z-frame gate, 112–113
Glue, polyurethane, 135
Grades, lumber, 24, 26

H

Hardware
    fence, 30
    gate, 15, 28–29, 118–119
Hinges, 29, 118, 134
Horizontal rail fence, 66–69

I

Infill
    cutting angled, 58
    dealing with obstacles, 60
    design, 107

gate, 110–117, 120
installation tips, 58
installing inset, 56–57
installing surface-mounted, 54–55
lumber type for, 24
sloped fences, 48–49
spacing, 58
Invisible dog fencing, 8

K
Kentucky rail fence, 102–103
Kickboard, 53

L
Lag screws, 39
Landscaping tools, 22–23
Latches, 28–29, 119
Lath fence, 7, 13
Lattice fence
building, 79–81
overhead lattice, 11
for privacy, 10–11
tops, 108
types, 80
Layout, 42–49
curved fences, 47
fence line, 42–46
sloped fences, 48–49
Layout tools, 18
Leaning fence, straightening, 130–131
Levels, 18–21, 33
Louvered fence, 11, 72–73
Low fences, 7
Lumber
grades, 24, 26
inspecting boards, 26
sizes, 24
types, 24–26

M
Machine bolt, 39
Marking, 32–33
Masonry, hanging a gate on, 119
Mason's line, 18, 42–44, 48
Materials
fasteners, 30
gate hardware, 28–29
lumber, 24–26
metal, 27

synthetic, 27
vinyl, 27
Measuring techniques, 32–33
Metal fence, 27, 88–91
Miters, cutting, 35
Mitersaw, power, 35
Mortise, through, 107
Mortise-and-tenon joints, cutting, 41
Mortised post-and-rail fence, 74–75

N
Nailing, 36–37
Nails, 30, 122
Noise control, 10
Notched post-and-rail fence, 68–69
Notches, cutting, 40

O
Obstacles, dealing with, 11, 60
Ornamental metal fence, 88–91

P
Paint, 138
Paneled gate, 116–117
Pet fencing, 8
Picket fence, 76–78
Pilot holes, 38
Pipe clamp, 112, 135
Plywood fence, 82–84
Post-and-rail fences
capped, 66–67
double, 102–103
mortised, 74–75
notched, 68–69
Post caps, 106
Posthole digger, 22
Posts
adding, 124–125
anchoring to patio or deck, 46
digging postholes, 43
marking postholes, 43
notched, 40, 68–69
plumbing and aligning, 44
replacing, 126–127
sagging gate, 132–133
setting, 45–46
shoring up damaged, 128–129
stub, 128–129
in tamped earth and gravel, 46
trimming, 87

Prefabricated panel fence, 86–87
Pressure-treated lumber, 25–26
Privacy, fencing for, 10–11
Property line, locating, 6

R
Rail joints, 106–107
Rails
edge, 50–51
flat, 52–53
repairing, 122–123
segmented, 59
Rebar, 101
Reciprocating saw, 21, 103
Redwood, 25
Repairs, 122–136
gate, 134–136
posts, adding, 124–125
posts, replacing, 126–127
posts, sagging gate, 132–133
posts, shoring up, 128–129
rails, 122–123
straightening a leaning fence, 130–131
Rip cutting, 34
Rot, 129

S
Sag bar, 132–133
Saws
circular, 19, 34–35
mitersaw, 35
reciprocating, 21, 103
Scalloping, 78, 107
Scarf joint, 37
Screw eye, 131, 133
Screws
driving, 38
lag, 39
types, 30
Security fence, 8–9
Setting nails, 122
Shade, from fencing, 12–13
Shingle fence, 84
Siding fence, 82–85
clapboard, 84–85
plywood, 82–84
shingle, 84
tongue-and-groove, 84–85
Slat fencing, 7

Sloped fences, 11, 48–49
Snow fences, 13
Solid-core gate, diagonal, 114–115
Solid fences
    building, 62–64
    for noise control, 10
    for privacy, 10–11
    for security, 8–9
Spacer, 58, 65, 67, 70, 72–73, 112
Squares, 19–20, 32–33
Squaring a gate, 134–135
Stains, 137–138
Stepped fencing, 48–49
Stops
    fence, 56–57, 71
    gate, 120
    lattice panel, 81, 117
Straightening a leaning fence, 130–131
Strike bar, 119
Stub post, 128–129
Swimming pool fences, 9
Synthetic fencing, 27, 92–95

T
T-bevel, 21, 113
Tenons, 75
Tension band, 98
Tension bar, 98
Toenailing, 37
Tongue-and-groove siding, 84–85
Tools
    caring for, 23
    construction, 18–21
    landscaping, 22–23
    layout, 18
    renting, 23
Top rail, 52–53
Top, style, 108
Trim, gate, 115
Turnbuckle, 132–133, 136

U
Utility lines, locating, 7
UV filtering agent, 137

V
Varnish, 137
Vertical board fence
    board-and-batten, 64
    board-on-board, 65

    gates, 64
    solid board, 62–64
Vinyl fences, 27, 92–95
Virginia zigzag fence, 100–101

W
Wildlife, fencing out, 9
Winch, 131
Wind control, 13
Wood, 24–26. *See also* Lumber

Z
Z-frame gate, 112–113
Zigzag fence, 100–101
Zoning ordinances, 7

Welcome Home

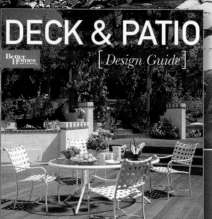

DECK & PATIO
[Design Guide]
Better Homes

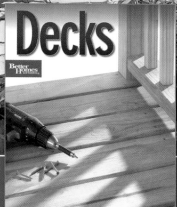

Decks
Better Homes

STEP-BY-STEP INSTRUCTIONS

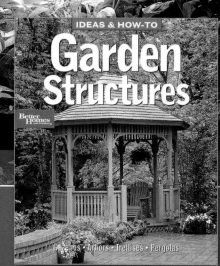

IDEAS & HOW-TO
Garden Structures
Better Homes and Gardens

Gazebos • Arbors • Trellises • Pergolas

Expert **advice** + **inspiration** + **ideas** + **how-to** for designing, building, maintaining your home's beautiful exterior

Better Homes and Gardens®

Fences & Gates

Helpful tips and techniques
Easy-to-follow instructions
Ideas and projects for your home

Popular fence projects

Time, skills, and tools needed to complete a project

BUILDING FENCES

Picket fence

■ **TIME:** Allow 2 or more days
■ **SKILLS:** Site layout, digging, concrete work, measuring and marking, cutting, fastening
■ **TOOLS:** Layout, digging, and concrete tools for layout and setting posts; carpentry tools for building fence

Picket fences are probably the most timeless and universal of all fence styles. They look equally stylish in a wide variety of landscapes, from Victorian to modern themes, augmenting the appeal of any landscape theme with their innate beauty.

HOW TO USE PICKET FENCES

■ Defining spaces: excellent; they clearly define any boundary with classic style
■ Security: moderate; they keep children and pets in or out, and pointed pickets can make it difficult to hop over
■ Privacy: none; open picket design permits open views
■ Creating comfort zones: minimal; low height does not block wind, but closely spaced pickets can block drifting snow

PICKET FENCE

Before you choose your picket style, visit your home center and look at preassembled 8-foot panels ready for installation. If you decide to save yourself some time with fence panels, make sure they are durable. Look for high-quality lumber (few knots and smooth finishes) and be wary of stapled frames. Millwork shops and some lumberyards will cut pickets for you for a fee, and of course you can cut your own designs too.

It doesn't matter whether you install the pickets on flush edge-rail or flat-rail frames, but if you like the looks of a flat-rail fence, you can add a kickboard to your design to minimize sagging. Most picket fences are installed on 4×4 posts and look best between 36 and 48 inches tall. Use 6×6 posts for fences taller than 5 feet (a taller fence starts to look like a stockade).

Before you put up a picket fence, experiment with picket widths and spacing to get the look you want. Traditional 1×3 or 1×4 pickets spaced 2½ to 3 inches apart will give you a classic look, but you can experiment to find spacing that pleases you. Draw fences to scale on ¼-inch graph paper.

First establish your bay width—6 to 8 feet is ideal. Then, to figure the picket spacing, decide how many pickets you want to spread across the bay. Multiply that number by the actual picket width and subtract the result from the bay width to find the total amount of open space. Divide this figure by a number one more than the number of pickets to find the distance between them.

1 Build the frame

Lay out the fence line with 6- to 8-foot bays, dig the holes, and set the posts with their tops 36 to 48 inches above the ground. Build flat-rail frames between the posts. Tack a batten 2 to 4 inches above the ground and use it to keep the bottom of the pickets on the same plane when you fasten them. Measure the distance between posts to compute the number of pickets you'll need to fill the bay. Recheck your measurements after installing the first few pickets and adjust the spacing if necessary.

Batten keeps pickets lined up.

2 Attach pickets

Distribute your pickets along the bay so they will be handy when you need them. Using the results of your computation for the number and spacing of the pickets, make a cleated spacer (page 58). Set each picket on the batten, space it with the spacer as shown, and fasten it to the rails.

76

77

Useful tips help ensure success

ISBN 978-0-696-23660-0

Detailed steps with clear photos and illustrations

U.S. $12.95

$14.95 in Canada

Visit us at bhgbooks.com